JIHAD
IN THE
ARABIAN SEA

HERBERT AND JANE DWIGHT WORKING GROUP
ON ISLAMISM AND THE INTERNATIONAL ORDER

*Many of the writings associated with this
Working Group will be published by the Hoover Institution.
Materials published to date, or in production, are listed below.*

ESSAYS

Saudi Arabia and the New Strategic Landscape
Joshua Teitelbaum

Islamism and the Future of the Christians of the Middle East
Habib C. Malik

Syria through Jihadist Eyes: A Perfect Enemy
Nibras Kazimi

The Ideological Struggle for Pakistan
Ziad Haider

BOOKS

Freedom or Terror: Europe Faces Jihad
Russell A. Berman

The Myth of the Great Satan: A New Look at America's Relations with Iran
Abbas Milani

Torn Country: Turkey between Secularism and Islamism
Zeyno Baran

Islamic Extremism and the War of Ideas: Lessons from Indonesia
John Hughes

Crosswinds: The Way of Saudi Arabia
Fouad Ajami

The End of Modern History in the Middle East
Bernard Lewis

The Wave: Man, God, and the Ballot Box in the Middle East
Reuel Marc Gerecht

Trial of a Thousand Years: World Order and Islamism
Charles Hill

Jihad in the Arabian Sea
Camille Pecastaing

HERBERT AND JANE DWIGHT WORKING GROUP ON ISLAMISM AND THE INTERNATIONAL ORDER

JIHAD

IN THE

ARABIAN SEA

Camille Pecastaing

HOOVER INSTITUTION PRESS
STANFORD UNIVERSITY | STANFORD, CALIFORNIA

www.hoover.org

Hoover Institution Press Publication No. 612

Hoover Institution at Leland Stanford Junior University, Stanford, California 94305-6010

Map prepared by International Mapping, Ellicott City, Maryland.

First printing 2011
17 16 15 14 13 12 11   9 8 7 6 5 4 3 2 1

Manufactured in the United States of America

The paper used in this publication meets the minimum Requirements of the American National Standard for Information Sciences—Permanence of Paper for Printed Library Materials, ANSI/NISO Z39.48-1992. ⊗

Library of Congress Cataloging-in-Publication Data
Pecastaing, Camille.
Jihad in the Arabian Sea / Camille Pecastaing.
    p. cm.— (Hoover Institution Press publication ; no. 612)
Includes bibliographical references and index.
ISBN 978-0-8179-1374-8 (cloth : alk. paper)—
ISBN 978-0-8179-1376-2 (e-bk.)
1. Mandab, Strait of, Region—History. 2. Mandab, Strait of, Region—Politics and government. 3. Islam and state—Mandab, Strait of, Region. 4. Red Sea Region—History. 5. Red Sea Region—Politics and government. 6. Islam and state— Red Sea Region. I. Title.
DT39.P43 2011
967.7'032—dc23   2011018124

To Leo

HOOVER
INSTITUTION

STANFORD
UNIVERSITY

*The Hoover Institution gratefully acknowledges
the following individuals and foundations
for their significant support of the*

HERBERT AND JANE DWIGHT WORKING GROUP
ON ISLAMISM AND THE INTERNATIONAL ORDER:

Herbert and Jane Dwight
The Beall Family Foundation
Stephen Bechtel Foundation
Lynde and Harry Bradley Foundation
Mr. and Mrs. Clayton W. Frye Jr.
Lakeside Foundation

CONTENTS

F OR DECADES, THE THEMES of the Hoover Institution have revolved around the broad concerns of
political, economic, and individual freedom. The
cold war that engaged and challenged our nation during
the twentieth century guided a good deal of Hoover's work,
including its archival accumulation and research studies.
The steady output of work on the communist world offers
durable testimonies to that time and struggle. But there is
no repose from history's exertions, and no sooner had com-
munism left the stage of history than a huge challenge arose
in the broad lands of the Islamic world. A brief respite and
a meandering road led from the fall of the Berlin Wall on
11/9 in 1989 to 9/11. Hoover's newly launched project, the
Herbert and Jane Dwight Working Group on Islamism and
the International Order, is our contribution to a deeper
understanding of the struggle in the Islamic world between
order and its nemesis, between Muslims keen to protect the
rule of reason and the gains of modernity and those determined to deny the Islamic world its place in the modern
international order of states. The United States is deeply
engaged, and dangerously exposed, in the Islamic world,
and we see our working group as part and parcel of the
ongoing confrontation with the radical Islamists who have

declared war on the states in their midst, on American power and interests, and on the very order of the international state system.

The Islamists are doubtless a minority in the world of Islam. But they are a determined breed. Their world is the Islamic emirate, led by self-styled "emirs and mujahedeen in the path of God" and legitimized by the pursuit of the caliphate that collapsed with the end of the Ottoman Empire in 1924. These masters of terror and their foot soldiers have made it increasingly difficult to integrate the world of Islam into modernity. In the best of worlds, the entry of Muslims into modern culture and economics would have presented difficulties of no small consequence: the strictures on women, the legacy of humiliation and self-pity, the outdated educational systems, and an explosive demography that is forever at war with social and economic gains. But the borders these warriors of the faith have erected between Islam and "the other" are particularly forbidding. The lands of Islam were the lands of a crossroads civilization, trading routes, and mixed populations. The Islamists have waged war—and a brutally effective one, it has to be conceded—against that civilizational inheritance. The leap into the modern world economy as attained by China and India in recent years will be virtually impossible in a culture that feeds off belligerent self-pity and endlessly calls for wars of faith.

The war of ideas with radical Islamism is the central pillar of this Hoover endeavor. The strategic context of this clash is the landscape of that Greater Middle East. We face three layers of danger in the heartland of the Islamic world: states that have succumbed to the sway of terrorists in which state authority no longer exists (Afghanistan, Somalia, and Yemen), dictatorial regimes that suppress their people at home and pursue deadly weapons of mass destruction and adventurism abroad (Iraq under Saddam Hussein, the Iranian theocracy), and "enabler" regimes, such as the ones in Egypt and Saudi Arabia, which export their own problems with radical Islamism to other parts of the Islamic world and beyond. In this context, the task of reversing Islamist radicalism and of reforming and strengthening the state across the entire Muslim world—the Middle East and Africa, as well as South, Southeast, and Central Asia—is the greatest strategic challenge of the twenty-first century. The essential starting point is detailed knowledge of our enemy.

Thus, the working group will draw on the intellectual resources of the Hoover Institution and Stanford University and on an array of scholars and practitioners from elsewhere in the United States, the Middle East, and the broader world of Islam. The scholarship on contemporary Islam can now be read with discernment. A good deal of it, produced in the immediate aftermath of 9/11, was not particularly deep and did not stand the test of time and events. We, however, are in the favorable position of a "second generation" assessment of that Islamic material. Our scholars and experts can report in a detailed, authoritative way on Islam within the Arabian Peninsula, on trends within Egyptian Islam, and on the struggle between the Kemalist secular tradition in Turkey and the new Islamists, particularly the fight for the loyalty of European Islam between those who accept the canon, and the discipline, of modernism and those who don't.

Arabs and Muslims need not be believers in American exceptionalism, but our hope is to engage them in this contest of ideas. We will not necessarily aim at producing primary scholarship, but such scholarship may materialize in that our participants are researchers who know their subjects intimately. We see our critical output as essays accessible to a broader audience, primers about matters that require explication, op-eds, writings that will become part of the public debate, and short, engaging books that can illuminate the choices and the struggles in modern Islam.

We see this endeavor as a faithful reflection of the values that animate a decent, moderate society. We know the travails of modern Islam, and this working group will be unsparing in depicting them. But we also know that the battle for modern Islam is not yet lost, that there are brave men and women fighting to retrieve their faith from the extremists. Some of our participants will themselves be intellectuals and public figures who have stood up to the pressure. The working group will be unapologetic about America's role in the Muslim world. A power that laid to waste religious tyranny in Afghanistan and despotism in Iraq, that came to the rescue of the Muslims in the Balkans when they appeared all but doomed, has given much to those burdened populations. We haven't always understood Islam and Muslims—hence this inquiry. But it is a given of the working group that the pursuit of modernity and human welfare, and of the rule of law and reason, in Islamic lands is the common ground between America and contemporary Islam.

IN ITS LEGEND, BAB EL-MANDEB ("Gates of Tears"), at the southern tip of the Red Sea, got its name from the multitudes who were drowned by the earthquake that separated Asia from Africa. In a more modern telling, the name had been given to this passageway by the dangers attending its navigation and the relentless winds that blow through it. Either way, the lands and coasts across Bab el-Mandeb and farther up have had a forbidding reputation. They have been lands of piracy and privation. Outsiders wandered into these ports, and often pushed into the interior, drawn there by strategic necessity and the imperatives of commerce, or by the competition of the Great Powers. But their footprint was always light, and they were, in the scheme of things, eager to leave this landscape to its own. Aden had once had its moment, a fueling station on the Suez-Bombay run. The British had staked a claim to it in 1839, and for nearly a century, it was governed as an outpost of the empire in India. It even became a Crown colony, and there were hints of British permanence. But Aden was given up when the *Pax Britannica* had grown weary of its burdens "east of Suez" in the late 1960s. In time, the hinterland behind Aden would claim this strategic outpost.

Only a brave scholar would venture into those domains. The writer would need an eye for the land itself—harsh and desolate—and for the tangled ethnicities, for the schemes of outsiders, and for the fierce resistance, and the cunning, of Yemenis and Somalis and Sudanese and Ethiopians alternately inviting outsiders into their affairs only to war against them. We are lucky that Camille Pecastaing has scholarly courage aplenty. His interests are eclectic; they span history and demography and economic and religious life and the rise and undoing of charismatic pretenders. It is perhaps more than an accident that he hails from France, which gave us the great scholar Fernand Braudel, whose inquiry into the Mediterranean world remains one of the scholarly enterprise's towering accomplishments. In the fashion of Braudel, who took in the whole world of the Mediterranean—the religions, the traffic of goods and men, the history of the olive tree, the play between mountains and plains—Professor Pecastaing takes us with him into Somalia and Yemen, the Sudan and Djibouti, with excursions into Ethiopia. All the things that truly matter in this wide swath of territory matter to him. There is a feel for the land, there is a seamless blend of history and current headlines, there is sympathy but no fawning for the peoples he studies. He makes his way through both history and geography, with beguiling grace.

The best kind of policy writings make their way, and meander, through geography and social and economic history and cultural anecdote. The world is illuminated, and there lies before us a subtle guide into the workings of a particular place and a particular people. This is the distinct advantage of this splendid book. Nowadays, Yemen concerns us—the possibility of its failure, the autocracy in the saddle that both breeds terror and poses as a gendarme against terror, the poverty of the land, and the scarcity of water. And Yemen is here, depicted with poise and detail. Somalia, too, is another challenge—a place that slipped out of statehood itself into mayhem and disorder. And in these pages there is a superb rendering of that tormented country. The bandits don masks—religious masks even—but the author knows the ways of pirates and piracy.

There is scholarly courage in this inquiry, to be sure. But there is also poise and discretion, and a knowledge of the dangers that await those who get caught in these straits of trouble.

Fouad Ajami

Senior Fellow, Hoover Institution
Cochairman, Herbert and Jane Dwight Working Group
on Islamism and the International Order

JIHAD
IN THE
ARABIAN SEA

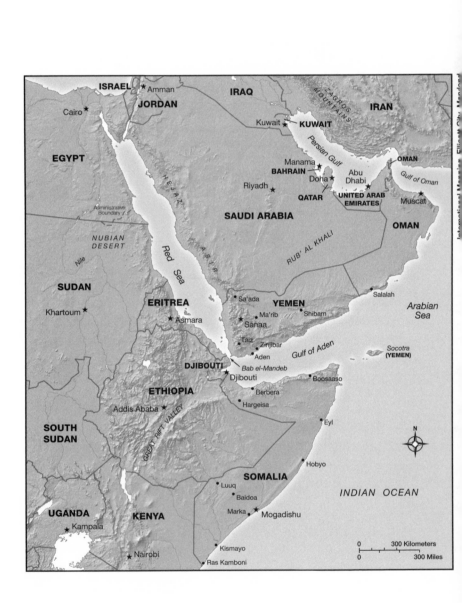

CHAPTER ONE

The Gates of Tears: Two World Orders

THE BAB EL-MANDEB, the strait that separates the Red Sea from the Indian Ocean, has conjoined Africa and Asia for centuries. It likely was the first route taken by *Homo sapiens* on their journey out of Africa, and the traffic between the Horn and Arabia has continued apace to this day. Men, goods, and ideas have gone back and forth, giving the Arabian Sea a degree of integration and similarity that is obfuscated by the arbitrary taxonomy of modern geography: Africa vs. Asia; the Horn of Africa vs. Arabia vs. South Asia. Only some 3,300 kilometers (about 1,800 nautical miles) separate Mumbai from Djibouti, the extreme range of a series of seaports and islands that dot the Arabian Sea: Massawa, Djibouti, Aden, Berbera, Mogadishu, Socotra, Muscat, Hormuz, Gwadar, Karachi, Mumbai.

The harsh, unforgiving environment is another factor of uniformity, as is the seasonal rhythm of the monsoon winds, which influences cattle migrations, harvests and, back in the era of sailboats, the coming and going of merchants. And there is *khat*, a shrub grown on the plateaus of

Ethiopia and Yemen whose leaves are chewed ubiquitously by the locals for its euphoric properties and for suppressing appetite in times of famine. Given its central location in the Eurasian trade route for at least the past 2,500 years, the region has been continuously exposed to the flux of historical change, to new ideas and technology passing through. Yet, the ancient states that once existed—the Sabean kingdom, Aksum—passed and were not replaced. Major civilizations are born on the beds of large rivers, but the lands that skirt the Gulf of Aden and the Arabian Sea have run dry, an arid belt stretching from the Nile to the Indus.

The environment has continuously degraded over the millennia, partly as a result of local climate change, partly due to human activity. The wooded hills have given way to rocky crags, the meadows turned into dust bowls. Both shores of the Bab el-Mandeb are among the hottest places on earth. Water is mostly found in the aquifer that is slowly being depleted; the rivers of the rainy season do not reach the sea. For most of the past 1,000 years, the lack of natural resources has allowed only light population density, minimal capitalization, and sporadic political centralization. Nomadic tribalism and sparse settlements have been a dominant form of social organization, with the occasional rise of a monarchic dynasty that never quite had it to evolve into more permanent forms of statehood.

These constraints were never lifted in the postcolonial era. Britain, France, and Italy ruled over the region lethargically and departed between the 1940s and the 1970s, leaving nominally independent states that proved to be of limited sustainability. Djibouti came to live off strategic rent paid by the United States and France. Somalia failed as a state in 1991, and has since eluded attempts to form a centralized polity. Yemen has been in a marginally better situation, using limited oil reserves to maintain a degree of political cohesion, which after thirty years of one-man rule has been worn down by both political and economic forces.

At the dawn of the twenty-first century, the challenges for the countries on the littoral of the Arabian Sea are civil war(s), piracy, radical Islamism, transnational terrorism, and a real risk of environmental and economic failure on both sides of the strait. Yet, its strategic importance as a conduit for maritime trade between Asia and the Mediterranean world is as great as it was when Egyptian pharaohs built a canal between the Nile and the Red Sea. Then, just as today, the lands around the Bab el-Mandeb were as difficult to pacify as the Red Sea was treacherous to navigate. The historical documents found in the Cairo Geniza show that in AD tenth century, vessels leaving Egypt sailed in a convoy along the route to India in order to deter a profusion of local pirates.

Islam came early to the region, during the life of the Prophet Muhammad, carried by small groups of refugees when the young Muslim community was still persecuted in Mecca. In the following centuries, Islam settled throughout the Indian Ocean amid the numerous merchant communities that thrived under the aegis of *Pax Islamica*. Arab Muslim traders would dominate that commerce for a thousand years, their *dhows* sailing from the mouth of the Red

Sea down the African coast to Malindi, in Kenya; across
the Arabian Sea to Mumbai and Goa, in India; through
the Strait of Malacca all the way to Canton, in South
China. Their activities were regulated by the commercial
law of the Sunni Shafi'i school of jurisprudence, which as
a result became dominant in the Indian Ocean. Sufi orders
expanded to form long-distance networks, providing travel-
ers with trusted local agents and housing facilities. Zheng
He, the legendary Chinese navigator of the fifteenth century, was a Muslim.

Muslim dominance of the maritime commerce in the
Indian Ocean continued until the seventeenth century.
Following Vasco da Gama's first trip to India, in 1498, the
Portuguese had forced themselves onto that ecosystem but
without changing much of its fundamental characteristics.
The Portuguese were pirates and petty traders in a world of
pirates and petty traders. Western supremacy came later,
with the Dutch and the British trading companies. Com-
mercial dominance led to political dominance, and the 1757
Battle of Plassey delivered Bengal to Robert Clive of the East
India Company. Muslim power was waning throughout the
Indian Ocean. The Mughal Empire, the world's richest
Muslim polity of the early modern period, a torchbearer
for Islam's secular power, was losing ground in the Indian
peninsula to British interests. Soon it was the turn of the
Muslim sultanates of the Southeast Asian archipelago (in
today's Indonesia and Malaysia) to pass under the protection of the Dutch and the British companies. The littoral
sultanates of the Arabian Peninsula (modern-day Yemen,

Qatar, Bahrain, Kuwait, and the United Arab Emirates)
would make similar arrangements with Britain in the early
nineteenth century. The coast of Muslim Africa was next.

The African continent produced ardent defenders of
Muslim sovereignty against European imperial expansion. In
1830, a French expeditionary corps was sent on a whim to
invade Algiers. And there stood Abd al-Kadir, the Algerian
Sufi shaykh who held the lines against the French Army—
not so long before, Napoleon's Great Army—for seventeen
years. The French would have to commit a vast contingent
and ravage the country to get him to surrender. They would
go on in their African ventures to build a canal between Suez
on the Red Sea and Port Said on the Mediterranean, which
in a roundabout way delivered Egypt and Sudan to the British. And there stood Muhammad Ahmad, the Sudanese
shaykh of the Samaniyah Sufi order and self-proclaimed
Mahdi ("messiah") who, in 1881, rose in rebellion against
Anglo-Egyptian rule. Muhammad Ahmad's followers—the
Ansars—famously massacred a British contingent led by
Maj. Gen. Charles Gordon at the 1885 Battle of Khartoum,
setting back the British claim over Sudan for thirteen more
years. While Abd al-Kadir was religiously moderate—and
would spend the rest of his days authoring poetry and religious exegesis—Muhammad Ahmad's call was already fundamentalist. The ferocity and determination of the Mahdi's
Ansars, attributed to their religious fanaticism, would
become the stuff of British colonial lore.

Abd al-Kadir and Mahdi Muhammad Ahmad were both
Sufi shaykhs. Sufism is a syncretistic form of Islam, which

reconciles a classical, monotheist Sunni theology with mystical, folkish practices, in particular the veneration of holy men. The Samaniyah order of Mahdi Muhammad Ahmad combined its Sufi orientation with elements of militant fundamentalism emerging in Arabia and south Asia from the mid-eighteenth century. This fundamentalist surge, propelled by global modernizing forces and Western encroachment in Muslim lands, has given the world new terms, or new meanings to old terms. *Salafism* refers to the legal doctrine that underpins the fundamentalist revival. Its principle is to eschew centuries of Islamic jurisprudence and refer back to the fundaments, the texts and records of the time of the Prophet. In practice, salafism proposed to withdraw legislative and judiciary authority from the Muslim empires and transfer them to a scholarly elite qualified to issue legal decisions: the *mujtahids*, the scholars who issue fatwas. The salafi preachers had a political agenda: in the name of tradition, they were proposing a politico-legal revolution.

Wahhabism, named after the Arabian scholar Muhammad ibn abd al-Wahhab, is the variance of salafism that emerged in Najd, a particularly arid region in the center of the Arabian Peninsula. Wahhabism was carried on the battlefields by several generations of the family of al-Saud, a local chieftain. In the early twentieth century, a scion of the Najdi clan finally implanted the faith at the core of a state-building project, in a kingdom that would bear his name. The proximity of Arabia brought the fundamentalist strain to Yemen, where it is already apparent in the career of Muhammad al-Shawkani. Al-Shawkani, a scholar who lived from 1760 to 1834, was a full generation younger than abd al-Wahhab (1703–1792). A revered cleric who would rise to be the highest religious authority in the Zaydi (Shia) imamate of north Yemen, al-Shawkani enlisted the salafi method, despite its roots in Sunnism, in support of the local dynasty, the al-Qasimi. A prolific writer, the author of Quranic exegesis and many legal decisions, he exemplifies the intellectual and legal rejuvenation salafism represented in those years.

Yet, neither salafism (reviving Islam) nor modernism (copying the West) could save the great Muslim empires, maladapted to the changing times. Following the ill-fated "Indian Mutiny" of 1857, the Moghul realm became the British Raj. In the crucial decades that followed, the Hindus and Muslims of India took different journeys to modernity, and the Muslims fell behind. For the large Hindu majority, politically subjected but numerically dominant, the British Raj was the opportunity to make new claims to power in the name of Western-like nationalism and of a democracy based on numbers. For the Muslims, for centuries a ruling minority in the realm, there was nowhere to go but down and many adopted nostalgic, reactionary attitudes that prevented them from formulating a coherent response to the changing circumstances. In 1947, the subcontinent was partitioned, leaving two regions in Punjab and Bengal for Muslims to live in an insular Muslim state that had no historical precedent. The new state of Pakistan would struggle for

decades after that to define the kind of society it was—
giving the salafis a shot at defining those terms and Islamiz-
ing the state. The Ottoman Empire, once the main power in Europe
and the seat of the Muslim caliphate, was by the 1920s
reduced to an Anatolian runt, fiercely Turkish and secular.
And so, in the latter half of the twentieth century, through
decades of heartbreak and soul-searching, salafism crystallized as a retrogressive, proselytizing undercurrent based on
modern imaginings of religious and political practices as
they may have existed in seventh-century Arabia. Da'awa is
the form of proselytism by which salafism is diffused, a
grassroots program centered on social work and on teaching
the proper rituals for an Islamic life. In the turbulent 1960s,
salafism fused with distinctly modern, revolutionary doc-
trines of armed struggle. Nationalism, nihilism, Marxism-
Leninism, even anarchism were cleansed of their atheist core
and recycled into a modern call to jihad. Jihadism became
"global" when it adopted, in the 1990s, a transnational strategic orientation, a determination to bring armed struggle to
the heart of Western nations.

Salafism, and Wahhabism in particular, vigorously
rejected Sufism as a form of idolatry. But in Africa, fundamentalism and Sufism managed to coexist: in Sudan, in
Somalia, and also in central Libya, which in the mid-
nineteenth century passed under the influence of the austere
Sanussiyya Sufi order. Then, just as today, fundamentalism
was an instrument of political mobilization that transcended tribalism and the multitude of interpersonal bonds

between local shaykhs (religious and tribal leaders) and their local clients. Sufism, on the other hand, bound an army of followers to a charismatic leader with supernatural powers, a man granted divine blessing to bring about radical and miraculous social change. Fundamentalism gave feelings of righteousness; Sufism of chosenness. The flirtation of the two, while doctrinally paradoxical, was in Africa a powerful force that could be harnessed for political and military purposes.

CHAPTER TWO

In the Land of the Mad Mullah: Somalia

EUROPEAN POWERS fell upon Africa in the nineteenth century. In the midst of the social dislocation of these times, in the space between the Arabia of Muhammad ibn abd al-Wahhab (the founder of Wahhabism) and the Sudan of Muhammad Ahmad (the Mahdi), on the Somali coast rose another nationalist hero with religious colors. Sayyid Mohammed Abdullah Hasan of the Darood clan was heir to both a warrior and a Sufi tradition, but he first embraced a religious and literary vocation. A poet and a scholar, he traveled for years in neighboring African countries to study Islamic theology. It was during a pilgrimage to Mecca in the early 1890s that he embraced the Salihiyya Sufi order, an upstart movement that had managed to combine the mysticism characteristic of Sufism with fundamentalist strains acquired in the proximity of the up-and-coming Wahhabi current.

Returning to preach in his native land of Somalia in 1895, Mohammed Abdullah Hasan found a noxious political context. Endemic rivalries between Somali clans had led local sultans to accept the protection of European powers. Small sultanates in northern Somalia (the future Somaliland) had passed under British influence; Italians were present in both Eritrea and in the Horn, and they were pushing down the coast toward Kenya and looking inland at Ethiopia; the French had a base in the Gulf of Tadjoura, as protectors of the two local tribes, one of which was Somali. Inland, the Ogaden, a vast plateau and grazing area for Somali pastoralists, was progressively absorbed by the expanding Christian kingdom of Ethiopia, with British acquiescence. Missionaries roamed the land where Islam, more of a cultural than a political presence, seemed ill-equipped to resist Christianization.

Mohammed Abdullah Hasan would confront the Christian powers militarily, rallying followers to a cause that was about the Muslim faith and about Somali honor and about his own personal mystique—a cause too imbued with magic perhaps to be nationalism, but something close to it. His fast-expanding groups of followers were called "Dervishes" by the British, a term used pejoratively to underscore their religious commitment. With weapons purchased from smugglers from the coast, the Dervish Army was to fight Britain, Ethiopia, and Italy for two decades. A Dervish State, built around the expanding Salihiyya order, would run parts of Somalia with rising and ebbing fortunes. It would endure until the end of World War I, when epidemics and the Royal Air Force decimated its ranks and its population centers. As for Mohammed Abdullah Hasan, the wanted man whom the British called the Mad Mullah, he would himself fall victim to the great influenza epidemic of 1920.

The demise of the Dervish State kicked off forty years of European rule. The Somali coast had been carved out among Britain, France, and Italy, none of which had much in terms of developmental projects for the region. Colonization was dormant, disturbed only when those foreign nations found themselves on opposite sides of the Second World War. Italy quickly lost its East African colonies to Britain, which at war's end was faced with the responsibility to craft the future of the region. For Somalia, independence would come in 1960, engineered under the auspices of the United Nations. The new Somali Republic was meant to be a centralized state, with its capital in the port city of Mogadishu, unifying the former British and Italian colonies. French Djibouti, however, was left to go its own way after a rigged vote. Britain had also allowed chunks of traditionally Somali land to pass to Kenya (a British colony) and Ethiopia (a British ally in World War II, which was also allowed to annex Eritrea). The loss of the Ogaden, an ethnically Somali heartland, now an Ethiopian province thrust like a wedge into western Somalia, marred the birth of the new state.

Somalia is ethnically, linguistically, and religiously homogenous. Somalis are Sunni Muslims, adherents to the Shafi'i legal tradition colored by the folkish, Sufi practice characteristic of agrarian societies. The Qadiriyyah Sufi order, historically well established all over Muslim Africa, coexists in Somalia with younger orders that emerged in the ferment of nineteenth-century Arabia, like the Idrisiyah, and the Salihiyya of Mohammed Abdullah Hasan. Following independence, the traditional Sufi orders were joined by new

forms of religious organization: Islamic da'awa movements,
local formulations of a model developed in Egypt in the
1930s by the Muslim Brotherhood, occasionally accentu-
ated by the more virulent strain of salafism that prevails
in Saudi Arabia. In the late 1960s, Wahdat al-Shabab al-
Islamiyya (Islamic Youth Union) was operating in northern
Somalia, while al-Jama'a al-Islamiyya (the Islamic Group)
was doing the same in Mogadishu and the south. They
occupied the religious end of the fragmented political landscape, reacting to the atheism of then-popular socialist ide-
ologies peddled by the secular parties.

Ethnic and religious homogeneity ended where tribalism—or, more exactly, tribalism in the context of the
Somali clan structure—began. In Somalia, clans were not
the obsolete legacy of history but the form of social organization adapted to a pastoral economy in an environment
with limited carrying capacity. Resources to support the
expensive structure of a state were lacking—most of the
population was nomadic and illiterate, the national economy centered on the export of livestock. Settled agriculture
was limited to the south, to banana fields along the marshy
beds of the Shebelle and Jubba rivers, and there was some
fishing and trade on the coast. Towns were havens for those
unable to withstand the harsh nomadic life: the elderly,
widows, and excess hands who subsisted on the petty commerce and charity of urban centers. With a population,
around the time of independence, at under 3 million, the
situation remained manageable despite the shallow economic base.

In the 1960s, tribalism was perceived as a thing of the past. Modernization, development, and a unified national identity were seen as the unavoidable model of social evolution. The only debate was about the form of political organization. A single-party system with state control of resources was fashionable at the time among the nationalist elites of late-developers, but Britain and the United Nations favored a multiparty system and market economy. Somalia was therefore born a democracy. Politics in 1960s Somalia mirrored those of other newly independent Arab and African democracies, with a vibrant if debilitating diversity built around a variety of competitors, traditional leaders and emergent elites with a Western education, vying for a share of the resources available to the new state. Electoral contingencies made it difficult to transcend the traditional claims of clans and political patrons.

The veneer of progress and the promise of modernization did not survive the 1960s. The fragmented political landscape encouraged elites to fight and paralyze each other. In a classic postindependence scenario, a military commander seized power in a 1969 bloodless coup. Mohamed Siad Barre was a modernist policeman. He had worked for the British colonial police and trained with the Italian *Carabinieri*. As a top-ranking cadre in the new Somali Army, he had also trained with Soviet officers and, once in power, he sought to impose a socialist model, with centralized governance and popular mobilization. Barre spoke of "scientific socialism" as a road to transcend clannish tribalism and rally the Somali nation around a common project. An undisputed autocrat, he felt he could have his way with the population. What his regime lacked in resources he would make up with ambition, authority, and wild optimism.

The one resource that Barre thought he could rely on in the context of the Cold War was strategic rent. Somalia has a long seashore along the Indian Ocean, with deep-sea ports in Berbera, Mogadishu, and Kismayo. Farther north, Aden and Djibouti strategically stand at the mouth of the Red Sea. Together, those ports control access to the Suez Canal and the Mediterranean. The Soviet Union, pursuing naval expansion in the 1970s, seemed happy to sign off on the ambitious programs of local clients in return for access to naval facilities. Aden, evacuated by the British in 1967, had passed under the control of a Moscow-friendly regime. Somalia would give Russia additional pieces in the geostrategic chess game.

If military aid could be expected from Russia, inspiration came from Morocco. In 1975, King Hassan II brought together a politically divided country by occupying the (hitherto Spanish) Western Sahara, a province allegedly lost by the Moroccan sultanate in the early days of Western imperialism. The Western Sahara affair was territorial expansion as a project for national development and unification, with a sprinkle of Islamic fervor. It did wonders for the Moroccan monarchy, granting its unloved king an extended lease on power in the name of national and religious pride. Somali national sentiments were running high in the 1960s and the 1970s. Somali irredentist groups had formed in Djibouti, Kenya, and Ethiopia. The lost Somali province of the Ogaden, given to Ethiopia by colonial fiat, would be Barre's Western Sahara.

The corruption of the court of Haile Selassie, the *negus* or "emperor" of Ethiopia, was legendary—although the legend owed, not in small part, to the scathing portrait of a delusional and autocratic ruler by Polish reporter Ryszard Kapuściński. Corruption led to moral and financial bankruptcy, and those sins came to light when a severe drought was followed by famine and food riots. People starved, but imperial dogs were fed delicacies. In 1974, troop mutinies spread throughout Ethiopia and the monarch was deposed by a military council, the *Derg*. Beyond the rioting, officers had also felt compelled to step in because secessionist and irredentist groups were threatening the territorial integrity of a state that had become accustomed to its imperial ambitions. There was at the same time a separatist insurgency in Eritrea; a newly formed Oromo Liberation Front seeking independence, even though the Oromos are the largest ethnic group in Ethiopia; and an irredentist group of Somalis in the Ogaden. Barre had a hand in the troubles in the Ogaden: he had been a source of weapons for the Ogadeni insurgents. In 1974, as Ethiopia plunged into chaos of its own making, members of the Somali National Army secretly crossed the border to reinforce the Western Somali Liberation Front. Together, they were taking out Ethiopian government outposts.

By a twist of fate, in early 1977, a colonel with Marxist credentials, Mengistu Haile Mariam, emerged as the leader of the *Derg*. Ethiopia under the negus had been a traditional ally of Great Britain and the West, but Mengistu sought to rebuild the country's position with an alliance with the Soviet Union. Barre responded by invading Ethiopia, in July 1977. It was no longer just about supporting rebels in the Ogaden: regular Somali troops quickly occupied most of the disputed region. At first, Moscow attempted to mediate a cease-fire between its allies, but when that failed, the decision was made to cut the supply lines to Somalia and rearm Ethiopia. Fortunes had turned. By March 1978, the Somali Army was forced to withdraw to its side of the border. The Ogaden War was over, its end the beginning of the end of the Somali state.

With Addis Ababa now anchored in the Warsaw Pact, Saudi Arabia brokered an arrangement for the provision of American military assistance to Barre. The whole region, one of the world's poorest, was awash with small arms and coming ablaze. Insurgencies in Eritrea, the Ogaden, south Sudan, and Oman were proxies in the great East-West engagement, each superpower concerned about conceding a geostrategic advantage. Some of those regional conflicts pitted Muslims against non-Muslims, but the battle lines were as often ethnic and personal as they were religious.

Despite Washington's military aid, the tide was turning against Barre. The costs of war, a growing population, and the mass of refugees driven out by the Ogaden War— Mengistu had used starvation to reestablish Ethiopia's authority—had exceeded the capacity of the government to cater to the needs of the people. Chief among the discontents were leaders of the Isaaq clan, dominant in the north, in the former British colony of Somaliland. The Isaaqs felt alienated by Barre's autocracy, shortchanged by a redistributive bias in favor of southern clans, and burdened by refugees from the war. Ogadenis were related to Barre's own clan, the Daroods, and many had found shelter in Isaaq territory, in the north. War tested the limits of Somali solidarity across clan lines. In 1981, in Jeddah, Isaaq leaders formed the Somali National Movement, an opposition group committed to the overthrow of the regime. Ethiopia offered its support.

Other Somali clans were also at odds with the autocrat. A 1978 coup attempt by military officers related to the Majerteen subclan had been answered with ethnic persecution from Somali Special Forces. In 1981, co-conspirators who had survived the crackdown formed an opposition group in Aden: the Somali Salvation Democratic Front, which recruited primarily from the Majerteen. Conflict between government and the various insurgents erupted on a large scale in 1982, and by 1986 Somalia had fragmented in a war between clan-based militias, as the Somali National Army came to rely on members of Barre's own Marehan faction and other groups that received the bulk of state patronage. The logic of clan identity and conflict tore at the fabric of Somali society. Civilians were harassed by virtue of their clan affiliation, suspected of sympathy for the rebels. In 1989, another insurgent group formed among the Hawiyes, one of the largest Somali clans.

The Isaaq-dominated Somali National Movement, with a sanctuary in Ethiopia and support from the Ethiopian government, was the most imposing adversary of the regime, and so repression fell heavy-handedly on the Isaaqs. Hargeisa, the regional capital, was razed by the Somali National Army. To drive a wedge between the rebels and their Ethiopian patrons, Barre conceded to Addis Ababa the Houd region, a grazing area in the Isaaq heartland that had been disputed for decades between Ethiopia and the colonial administrators of Somalia. All those efforts were in vain, and the twists and turns of history caught up with the autocrat. With the end of the Cold War, the flow of military aid to the region dried out, cutting off Somalia from the strategic rent it had come to depend upon. The civil war came to its logical conclusion in January 1991, when Mogadishu fell to the rebel faction from the Hawiye clan, the United Somali Congress. Barre's only consolation was that his nemesis, Ethiopian leader Mengistu Haile Mariam, abandoned by the Soviet Union, would be overthrown a few months later. But as Barre retreated west, to his clansmen homeland near the Ethiopian border, Somalia looked irredeemably partitioned into clannish fiefdoms.

The northernmost part of the country, where the Isaaq clan is dominant, was fully under the control of the Somali National Movement. Its leaders wasted no time in proclaiming the independence of the republic of Somaliland, resurrecting the former British protectorate. While the international community refused to recognize Somaliland, the insurgents reorganized in a political party that would administer the aspiring state with relative efficiency. The lack of international recognition meant that Somaliland was denied access to the benefits of sovereignty, its foreign assistance limited to a trickle. But something positive would come out of adversity. To improve its diplomatic standing, Somaliland has since organized multiparty elections that have led to actual transitions in power—a rare occurrence in the region. Eritrea is another young state, which earned its independence from Ethiopia the hard way. But with its sovereignty recognized by the international community in 1993, Eritrea was spared the necessity of a democratic life. Somaliland still has to earn its recognition.

Meanwhile, northeastern Somalia—the very tip of the Horn of Africa—had passed under the control of the Majerteen rebel faction, the Somali Salvation Democratic Front. A new administrative jurisdiction crystallized around the insurgent group, which would announce itself to the world in 1998 as Puntland—a reference to the mythical land of Punt. Puntland has since maintained a high level of autonomy, yet without claims to full independence. While the Majerteen subclan is strong in the administration of Puntland, the regional government is an alliance of local elders, bound to one another by a common desire to avoid the chaos that prevails in southern Somalia, but who do not share a state project. The region is not homogenous and has known tension between subclans. Puntland also lacks a common history as an administrative unit: it actually straddles the former British Somaliland and Italian Somalia. By eschewing independence, Puntland retained legal standing to receive a share of the foreign aid allocated to Somalia, and was spared the kind of international responsibility that comes with statehood. This compromise has worked relatively well for the province.

When Barre fell in 1991, the situation in the south was more complex than in the breakaway provinces of Somaliland and Puntland, in part because of Mogadishu. Mogadishu was too large and too diverse a city to fall under the control of one single clan or warlord. And Mogadishu was where the international community decided to start to rebuild the Republic of Somalia. The value of Mogadishu was both symbolic—as the capital of the defunct state—and material—as the deep-sea port where most foreign assistance was shipped to. The violence surrounding the collapse of the Barre regime had devastated Somali agriculture and livestock, and food aid was the only relief from the ongoing famine that would take the lives of a half-million. But aid, in the early 1990s, was routinely seized by local warlords and either used as a political instrument to build networks of patronage, or sold overseas. The proceeds could buy all forms of weapons from the Bakaraaha arms market in downtown Mogadishu.

The struggle for Mogadishu threw the Hawiyes in the limelight. Their clan is numerically dominant in Mogadishu and in the coastal region north of the capital, although the area is less homogenous clanwise than other parts of Somalia. In 1991–92, two factions were vying for control of the capital. Mohammed Farah Aidid's was the strongest. Aidid was much like the autocrat he had just deposed: a colonial policeman who had risen to the rank of general in postindependence Somalia, before going rogue as the leader of the

Hawiye United Somali Congress. But his success was short-lived. His movement had split, and his bid on power was opposed by the breakaway faction of Ali Mahdi Muhammad. Both were Hawiyes, but of different subclans, and Ali Mahdi had managed to steal the presidency from under Aidid's nose. Instead of Aidid rising to be the providential strongman around whom the international community hoped to rebuild Somalia, he and his rival warlord were trying to gain control over the flow of foreign aid to establish their hegemony.

Aid had become such high stakes in internal power struggles that, in December 1992, the United Nations sent military units to protect the relief mission, adding a layer of complexity to a volatile situation. The participation of American troops in the effort remained marginal, and was being scaled down when twenty-four Pakistani soldiers were killed in an ambush in June 1993. Aidid's militia was blamed for the killings, and that summer the United States sent a small contingent of Special Forces to take out the warlord and his lieutenants. This operation culminated in the infamous Battle of Mogadishu of October 3–4, 1993, when two American Black Hawk helicopters were shot down and 18 American soldiers killed. Several hundred Somalis were also killed, not only Aidid's militiamen but also many civilians caught in the cross fire.

The Battle of Mogadishu would have two consequences. In the short term, it made the position of the foreign mission in Somalia untenable—an American officer summed up the disillusionment with the entire undertaking: "We fed them. They grew stronger. They killed us." The operation would be shut down in the spring of 1995, long after the last U.S. troops had withdrawn. Famine was less pressing at the time, and the objective of rebuilding central authority seemed unachievable. In the long run, the withdrawal from Mogadishu fed the conviction that UN and U.S. troops always stepped down when engaged by a determined adversary. For the Americans, Mogadishu seemed a rerun of the withdrawal from Beirut after the terrorist attacks of 1983–84. For the UN, it was another episode in a growing list of failed missions. Two years later, in July 1995, UN troops would stand down to Serbian forces in Srebrenica, allowing the killing of 8,000 Muslim civilians.

Although unrelated incidents, the Battle of Mogadishu and the Srebrenica massacre would both feed suspicion in salafi milieus about the intentions of the international community toward Muslims. And maybe there was a relation after all. Seared by the debacle in Somalia, the Clinton administration had wearied of humanitarian interventions. It would take thirty months of slaughter in Bosnia and the massacre at Srebrenica to force American might into that war, in the summer of 1995. Reluctance built in Somalia to commit ground troops meant that only air power would be committed in the defense of Muslim Bosnians. The same reluctance was evident in Kosovo, in 1999, when NATO intervened on the side of Albanian populations against Serbian forces. Twice, NATO had imposed on Serbia to protect Muslims, but there would be no gratitude from the salafi milieus. Following the Dayton Accords, which brought reprieve to Bosnia, Western powers requested that the Muslim government in Sarajevo deport foreign jihadists, in fact exporting radicalism to other places. The simpler times when UN peacekeepers and foreign missions could stop a conflict by their mere presence were over.

Ethiopia had greatly contributed to the 1991 downfall of Mohamed Siad Barre, and it appeared to be the beneficiary of the conflict between warlords that raged in southern Somalia. But Ethiopia was also hurting; it had just lost the province of Eritrea and, with it, its only maritime access to the Red Sea. Ethiopia's maritime commerce was now entirely dependent on arrangements with Djibouti, and secondarily on access to the port of Berbera, in Somaliland. Although the ruling faction in Somaliland had been a client of Ethiopia since the civil war, the province and the port of Berbera were still legally part of Somalia. And Djibouti was a narrow corridor to the sea squeezed between Eritrea and Somalia, both of which were hostile to the landlocked state. Then, there was the undying problem of the Ogaden, around which the Ethiopian-Somali border runs for 1,600 kilometers (1,000 miles), too long to be guarded effectively. A weak, divided, dependent Somalia with Somaliland as a client state was for Addis Ababa a guarantee that its neighbor could never support its claims to the Ogaden, or squeeze off its access to the sea. To achieve that goal, Ethiopia kept nurturing friendly Somali factions against those who could pose a threat.

The threat came from a militant, fundamentalist outfit named Al-Ittihad al-Islami (the Islamic Union). The origins

of Al-Ittihad are found in the salafi da'awa movements of
the late 1960s. While still marginal in Somalia, those movements had established a small base of followers over the
years. Graduates of religious programs in Saudi Arabia or
Egypt, recipients of generous scholarships afforded by the
oil wealth, were reaching out to the population through
prayer groups and associative, grassroots work. At some
point between 1982 and 1984, amid the decay of the Barre
regime, two main salafi movements came together as Al-
Ittihad, which recruited young Somalis for the jihad against
the Soviet Union in Afghanistan. Although their numbers
were never as important as the contingents levied from
countries like Egypt and especially Yemen, the Somali
mujahideen learned new skills and orientations.

By the time the Somali state disintegrated in 1991,
Al-Ittihad had evolved into an armed, militant group. It
made a bid for power, proclaiming an Islamic emirate but
the beginnings were difficult. In Somaliland and Puntland,
Al-Ittihad militiamen clashed with and were quickly routed
by the local insurgent groups. By 1992, the Islamist militias
had fallen back to the town of Luuq, in the Gedo province,
west of Mogadishu, where they eventually controlled several
positions along the Ethiopian border. In Gedo, Al-Ittihad
carved a niche for itself picking up the flame of Somali
nationalism. From 1994, the campaign to liberate the
Ogaden had been renewed by the Islamists with border
raids and attacks deep into the contested region of Ethiopia.
The leader of Al-Ittihad, Hassan Dahir Aweys, was a natural: born in 1935, he was a career officer, a former colonel

in the Somali Army and a veteran of the Ogaden War. There were rumors of funding from supportive Saudis channeled through Somali businessmen in Kenya. Eritrea, still reeling from its own brutal war for independence and Ethiopia's archenemy, was also widely suspected of supplying the new combatant group.

Addis Ababa tried to contain the challenge of Al-Ittihad with air raids and local proxies. It provided support to rival warlords and clan leaders, as a result of which Al-Ittihad remained holed up in Gedo. But Ethiopia could not protect its long border against incursions, and it struggled with domestic liberation fronts that were reinforced by the Somali Islamists. Gedo was strategically convenient for Al-Ittihad: it is a tri-border area (Ethiopia-Kenya-Somalia), not too distant from the seaport of Kismayo, allowing for the movement of weapons and personnel from the coast into the Ogaden. In 1996, Ethiopian troops finally crossed into Somalia to dislodge the Islamists. Al-Ittihad could not hold on to their stronghold in the town of Luuq and retreated to the highlands. There were retaliatory bombings in Addis Ababa. The insurgency raged on until 1998, at which point Ethiopia and Eritrea became consumed in a costly border conflict that would last until 2000. It was real, open warfare: military against military, with artillery barrages and tens of thousands of casualties. Cut off from its supply lines, Al-Ittihad's fighters took advantage of a truce to scatter. The movement, effectively defunct, would disband in the wake of the 2001 attacks against the United States.

Al-Ittihad had been a regional phenomenon, contained to the border area, which by the end of the 1990s seemed to have run its course. Hassan Dahir Aweys resettled in Mogadishu. The Somali capital had been transformed during those years, as order had been rebuilt from the ground up in the unexpected guise of Shariah, or Islamic, courts. The courts had begun to operate in the chaos of the early 1990s, expanding their activity from traditional judicial functions (like the application of family law) to policing and the organization of basic social services, such as schools, clinics, and trash collection. The courts were supported by local merchants, who needed a modicum of order to operate their businesses, and by users, as a fee-based service. The courts lived side by side with local warlords, in a pragmatic relationship of convenience. Warlords could buy the loyalties of retainers with the proceeds of trafficking, but they could not relate to the people and organize local communities the way shaykhs could.

The first court to make a name for itself got started in north Mogadishu in 1994. It was run by Shaykh Ali Mohammad Raghe ("Dheere"), a Murusade-Hawiye, under the protection of the warlord and then-President Ali Mahdi Muhammad, a Abgal-Hawiye, whose rival, Mohammed Farah Aidid, a Habar Gidir-Hawiye, was an outspoken critic of Islamists. Shaykh Ali Dheere's fundamentalist inclinations provided him with an effective method to restore order in the war-torn capital: religious terror. While at the time unusual in Somalia, his extreme application of Islamic justice was effective, and the cleric grew in popularity and power as security and quality of life improved in the area under his control. Soon, there were a few other courts, which began to cooperate with one another, and militiamen gravitated toward them. Their power expanded at the expense of the warlords, who tried too late to disband them. Ali Muhammad, who had used Dheere against Aidid, was eclipsed by Dheere. All three men were from different sub-clans of the Hawiyes, a distinction that nourished factionalism in Mogadishu. Dheere's brand of Islamism was a way to transcend narrow affiliations and rally supporters.

The warlords were on a course of self-destruction. In 1995, Ali Mahdi surrendered the title of president to his rival Mohammed Farah Aidid. In 1996, "President" Aidid was assassinated. His son, Hussein Mohammed Aidid, a U.S. citizen and former Marine, briefly took over the presidential function. But the young man could not stake a claim to the country. It was the end of the warlords' era. With Aidid dead, courts sprouted in south Mogadishu. Momentum was on the side of the courts, which by 1996 were coordinating their operations across the capital. While Hawiyes, the majority population in Mogadishu, were dominant in the system, the courts were able to use the common factor of Islam to adjudicate disputes between the clans and sub-clans present in the mixed urban areas. Shaykhs could reach out to one another and come together where warlords only fought for turf and fragmented into ever-smaller units. It is this new world that Aweys, the leader of the insurgent group Al-Ittihad, found in Mogadishu in the late 1990s.

Al-Ittihad and the Shariah courts shared common origins in the past decades of salafi and Wahhabi proselytizing in Somalia. Salafism had never really been able to break through until the chaos that followed the fall of Siad Barre had given the fundamentalists the opportunity to deploy their organizational potential. Al-Ittihad was a combatant outfit, driven by its military purpose and the fortunes of war, and more of an umbrella for militants and commandos tethered to Eritrean support than a centralized organization with an independent resource base. The courts, on the other hand, were a bottom-up, decentralized phenomenon, driven by a social function, feeding from the society, and coming together on the basis of compromise and cooperation. Both developments occurred in parallel, and both expressed the fundamentalist strain, but they remained unrelated in numerous other ways.

Ethiopia was unimpressed by the distinction between Al-Ittihad and the Shariah courts, and it worked to undermine the new regime in Mogadishu. After a feat of diplomatic window dressing—a 2000 regional peace conference in Djibouti brokered by Ethiopia—Addis Ababa assembled personalities hostile to the courts into a Transitional Government, which received the blessing of the international community. It was a sham: men without power, marginalized warlords were legitimized as representatives of the nonexistent state of Somalia, members of a government that will, for years, live parasitically in regional resorts, its budget a minibar tab that often had to be picked up by the European Union. The Transitional Government was simply Ethiopia's latest proxy in the war-torn country, an antithesis to the Islamist state emerging on the ground.

Ethiopia's ability to manipulate the situation in Somalia owed to its superior diplomatic skills. First, Addis Ababa enjoyed a historically central role in the African Union—to the great chagrin of Eritrea, still embroiled in a boundary dispute with its former sovereign. Second, Ethiopia was a Christian-majority state, whose diplomatic hand was strengthened by the religious card in light of growing concerns in the international community over Islamist terrorism. In the 1990s, when Al-Ittihad was most active, no one beyond its immediate area of operations paid much attention to it. But, rightly or wrongly, the activity of Islamist terrorists in the region at the turn of the century tainted perceptions of what was happening in Somalia. In the fall of 2001, an executive order issued by the U.S. government would publicly associate Aweys and Al-Ittihad with the global jihad phenomenon. And from there, there was a trail leading from Aweys to the Shariah courts.

Between 2000 and 2004, local Shariah courts had gone from cooperating with each other to federating as an Islamic Courts Union. The growing authority of the proto-government of the Courts Union exposed the pretense of the Ethiopian-backed Transitional Government. Under circumstances that will be discussed in a subsequent chapter, warlords associated with the Transitional Government responded with a military alliance of their own, which started to clash with the courts in early 2006. Aweys had become involved with the courts in Mogadishu, bringing to the table more than twenty years of combat experience, his long-standing connection to Eritrea, and the remnants of Al-Ittihad. Aweys had organized the various courts' militias into a more cohesive military force, and when violence flared in early 2006, he led his men to a crushing victory

over the warlords. By June, they had taken control of
Mogadishu. The airport, closed since 1995, was reopened in
July. The seaport opened in August. Business even slowed
down in the Bakaraaha arms market, which had supplied
the warlords for over a decade.

The military arm of the Courts Union quickly moved
south and took the seaport of Kismayo. This success won
over the powerful warlord Yusuf Mohammed Siad (*Inda'ade,*
or "White Eyes"), who at the time controlled the densely
populated province surrounding Mogadishu. After that,
success kept coming. Islamist militiamen moved north and
took the port of Hobyo from the pirates. Some order had
returned to Somalia, and it was good for business. The only
section of the south that remained beyond the control of
the Islamic Courts Union was a sliver of land along the
Ethiopian border, including the town of Baidoa, under the
protection of the Ethiopian-backed Transitional Federal
Government.

Aweys was appointed head of the Shura Council of the
Islamic Courts Union; the warlord Yusuf Siad Inda'ade, rallied to the courts, became the head of security. The public
face of the Courts Union, its political leader, was the young
Sharif Sheikh Ahmed, a clean-looking cleric trained in
Sudan and Libya, and the local head of the Idrisiyah Sufi
order. Ahmed, then in his thirties, had returned to Somalia
in the late 1990s and risen through the Shariah courts. The
success of the Courts Union in mid-2006 suddenly presented southern Somalia with the prospect of restoration
of order under an Islamist cloak, with Shariah courts and

religious madrassas in lieu of public institutions. For some, this was an improvement over the anarchy of the warlord era; for others, it was the constitution of a Taliban-like emirate. In some areas, the courts were flying the fundamentalist colors: music was banned, women were forced to veil, and public criticism was silenced as if it were an attack on religious orthodoxy. The *hudud*—the brutal punishments of Islamic law that had made Shaykh Ali Dheere a power player—were applied in the public space.

Segments of Somali society learned to live with the fundamentalist religious attitudes; their security depended on the existence of religious militias. But that did not mean Somalia had caught the Al Qaeda strain of the fundamentalist bug. And the two phenomena—salafism and militias—were not always linked. Harakat al-Islah, a group in the Muslim Brotherhood tradition (a milder, Egyptian form of salafism), had made significant inroads in Mogadishu. With financial support from Saudi Arabia, Al-Islah runs local madrassas and introduced conservative practices common in Arabia, such as female veiling. Al-Islah is an indigenous, grassroots da'awa movement that spans the social spectrum of Somalia and transcends clannish boundaries in the name of a common Islam. It has a revisionist agenda, vested in the creation of an Islamic state that would reunite all the Somali provinces. But Al-Islah remains nonviolent in its methods.

Cultures continuously evolve, and given the intensity of challenges to leading a normal existence in Somalia since the 1980s, it is not surprising that cultural adaptation would be rapid and significant. An interesting subculture appeared among the Somali youth, provocatively blending jihadist themes with hip-hop as a vehicle for the expression of teenage angst. Somalia had gone through a degree of Islamization that departed from its traditions, but the visibility of more rigid Islamic strains does not mean salafism is uncritically accepted either. The Sufi orders still have a claim on segments of society, and they can respond to the salafi challenge by leveraging clannish and local affiliations. And then there are non-negotiable behaviors: Somalis are used to their tobacco and their khat, which cheer up the long, hot days. Salafis have tried to ban those substances at their own peril. Like any culture, Somalia is full of contrasts, pretenses, and smoke screens.

The social and economic reality of Somalia after years of statelessness is difficult to fathom in an age where modern states have such an extensive reach. The Islamic Courts Union owed its success to its ability to provide public goods and services—its power symbolically and practically peaked when Mogadishu finally had a running airport and seaport. Madrassas often are the only venue for education. Somali businessmen—the modern version of a mercantile class—have managed to operate despite the lack of a central government, providing the population with everything from oil to cellular service, from clothing to electronics, and all sorts of weapons from the Bakaraaha market, the world's largest open-air market for small arms. There are even hotels in Mogadishu. This activity requires a degree of order and protection which could be more easily obtained from a central force like the Islamic Courts Union than by local warlords, one neighborhood at a time.

In the absence of national economic statistics, analyzing the ability of Somalia to pay for imported goods is a bit of guesswork, but the issue is crucial, as most items come from abroad. The traditional agricultural base of exporting livestock to Arabia recovered in the mid-1990s, and Somalia also exports charcoal—a profitable but environmentally detrimental activity. The economic life revolves around the four seaports. Somaliland has Berbera; Puntland has Boosaaso; and the south has Mogadishu and Kismayo. In the south, when security permits, the ports are where vital shipments of foreign aid from international organizations such as the World Food Program, as well as aid from Islamic charities, are delivered. Beyond aid, Somalis survive on the remittances and donations from the mass of Somali refugees and expatriate workers in Kenya, Yemen, the United Arab Emirates, and beyond. The banking system had collapsed, but transfers are performed by a thriving, informal financial sector with reaches into the diaspora. Somali gangs also managed to extract protection payments from foreign trawlers fishing in the rich Somali waters, a lucrative activity that evolved into outright piracy. Despite its limitations, this stateless economy of 10 million people has shown remarkable resilience, rebuilding itself from the ground up.

CHAPTER THREE

In the Land of the Imam: Yemen

YEMEN'S HISTORY is the history of the Arab tribes, and beyond that, the history of humanity out of Africa. Even Yemen's own, idiosyncratic history goes as far back as the twelfth century BC, when the land that would be known as *Arabia Felix* for its lushness saw one civilization after another flourish. Yemen was blessed with fertile highlands, to which altitude brought regular rainfall, and a vast network of irrigation canals. A 580-meter-wide dam was erected in Ma'rib in the eighth century BC, under Sabaean rulers, to retain water through the dry season. Yemen also had a comparative advantage in rare crops, such as frankincense and myrrh resin used for religious rituals throughout the Mediterranean world. Caravans from south Arabia crossed the desert to the market ports of the Levant, carrying ivory and rare woods from East Africa, precious resins from Dhofar and the Hadramawt.

Yemen was touched by the first wave of Islam, during the lifetime of the Prophet. But the singularity of Yemen's religious history came from the establishment in the ninth century of a Zaidi imamate in Sa'ada, a city in the northern highlands. Zaidism is a form of Shiism that has remained into the twenty-first century the dominant faith in northern Yemen and in the southwestern province of Saudi Arabia. The fortunes (and the degree of independence) of the imamate ebbed and flowed across the centuries, but the region was remote, and never rich enough for the vast empires that claimed the Islamic caliphate to make sustained efforts to conquer it. In the Middle East, altitude, backwardness, and inaccessibility have made sanctuaries for religious minorities.

In the sixteenth century, the up-and-coming Ottoman Empire staked a claim on Arabia, although Istanbul's suzerainty was only strong on the coast. A new dynasty of Zaidi imams—the Qasimis—thrived in the highlands on the back of the prosperity brought to the region by Ottoman peace. For two centuries, the port of Mocha in the Tihamah supplied the world with *Arabica*—Arabian coffee. Maritime commerce in the Red Sea and the Indian Ocean was protected by the Muslim empires, and merchant ships from Surat in Gujarat (India) called regularly at Mocha. The coffee boom ended when Dutch merchants took the African bean to Java and Suriname, and within a few years cornered the European coffee market. Mocha's fortunes endured until the mid-eighteenth century, at which point it started a decline that a century later would reduce the city to ruins.

The Tihamah is the arid coastal plain that runs along the Red Sea from the Gulf of Aqaba to the Bab el-Mandeb, one of the hottest, most forbidding places on earth. Upland from Mocha and blessed with a cooler climate is Sanaa, a historical capital settled for the past 2,500 years. Sanaa, and to the north, the Zaidi political capital of Sa'ada, thrived during the coffee boom. This past prosperity is visible in the architecturally unique mud-brick high-rises in the Old City of Sanaa. Further east is the ancient city of Ma'rib. From there, on a north and south axis from the Arabian desert to the sea, runs the fertile heart of classical Yemen: the once-irrigated valleys of the Sabaean kingdom. Farther in the east, the Hadramawt is a vast universe of its own, sparsely populated, with a unique landscape of canyons and oases that carries through to the Dhofar region in Oman, to which it is adjacent. Somewhat insular yet attached to the outside world through its maritime shore—merchant communities of Hadrami origins dot the Indian Ocean all the way to Indonesia—the Hadramawt has retained a unique culture imbued with Sufism. This legacy will find an expression with the opening in the 1990s of a center for the study of Sufism—Dar al-Mustafa—that has caught worldwide attention. Like Sanaa, the ancient city of Shibam, once capital of an independent Hadrami kingdom, displays its past wealth with a unique architecture of mud-brick towers that go back to the sixteenth century.

Yemen presents a fragmented human and natural landscape. While the northern highlands are the base of a Zaidi culture that had long remained parochial, the coastal plain along the Red Sea and the south are home to a Sunni majority. Sunnism in Yemen is of the Shafi'i school, dominant throughout the Indian Ocean region and by vocation oriented to commerce. And there are the tribal divisions. Tribes in Yemen tend to be sedentary, especially in the more fertile south and in the eastern valleys, which have supported agricultural settlements for thousands of years. The trajectory of the Zaidi imamate shows that tribes accepted embryonic statehood when the local economy was favorable, although Yemen has rarely been rich enough since the beginning of the Islamic period to sustain statehood over the long term.

When times got tough and central institutions could no longer be maintained, the social system reverted to tribalism. In the north, the two main tribal confederations are the Hashid and the Bakil. In the south, the Himyar and the Maddhij trace their origins three millennia, to the legendary Semitic Qahtans—according to tradition, the forebears of modern Arabs. Tribalism is somewhat less pronounced in the south because of the solvent effect of sedentary agriculture, and of intermingling with populations that came to the coast: Turks, Africans, and other Arabs. In the east, tribal divisions mirror the mountainous geography that separates valleys from one another, with limited communication even in the twenty-first century. There is social fragmentation there, and the interaction between neighbors is often violent, unmediated by government authority and the rule of law.

In 1918, the demise of the Ottomans allowed for the establishment of what was, in the Westphalian context of the twentieth century, an independent Zaidi state: the

Mutawakkilite Kingdom of Yemen. The imam was now monarch, his kingdom spread over the northern area of modern Yemen. The south and the coast had passed from Turkish to British sovereignty. Back in 1839, the East India Company had plucked the derelict coastal village of Aden from the Sultan of Lahej. Later, under the control of the viceroy in India, the coaling and trading station of the East India Company grew into a naval base from which Britain flexed its maritime power. The Red Sea and Arabian Sea had to be cleared of their traditional ecosystem of piracy, smuggling, gunrunning, and slave trading. With the opening of the Suez Canal in 1869, Aden became a port of call on the India route, a crucial outpost of *Pax Britannica*. Aden was necessary to guard the sea-lanes, and then the hinterland became necessary to guard Aden. London signed protection agreements with the Sultans and tribes in the surrounding areas, cutting a zone of British influence in South Yemen and the Hadramawt.

Modern Yemeni history accelerated in the 1960s. It all started in the northern kingdom, where hereditary succession to the Zaidi imamate was halted in 1962 by a coup plotted by a Nasserist officer who sought to impose a socialist republic. Egypt, then a client of the U.S.S.R., sent more than 50,000 troops in support of the republican camp, which compelled Saudi Arabia to back the Zaidi tribes loyal to the monarchy. The Sunni-Shia religious lines were secondary to the ideological conflict. This was a piece of the Cold War and a battle between the two great Arab leaders of the era: Gamal Abdel Nasser and Prince, soon to be King,

Faisal ibn Abdul Aziz al-Saud. Stalemate ensued a period
of intense violence, with casualties in excess of 100,000. A
compromise of sorts was reached in 1968, as the royalist
tribes integrated a parliamentary system that had lost its
most radical, socialist edge. In 1970, Saudi Arabia acknowledged the establishment of a Yemen Arab Republic that
became, for all intents and purposes, dependent on Riyadh's financial largesse. The capital of the northern republic
was established in Sanaa, a more active and cosmopolitan
city than the northern Zaidi historical capital of Sa'ada.

As Saudi Arabia reluctantly built a republican semipro-
tectorate in the north, Britain was busy disengaging from
its protectorates in the south. The official announcement
that Britain would close all its bases "east of Suez" was
made by Prime Minister Harold Wilson in 1967, but troubles had been brewing for a while in South Yemen. Aden,
with its unionized dockhands and where all sorts of interlopers transited on their way east or west, had caught the
Nasserist bug, which spread to the nearby provinces. With
a full-fledged war raging in the north, small arms were not
hard to get and local insurgencies had flared in southern
tribal areas back in 1963.

The general British project for rolling back imperial com-
mitments was to bring together various sultanates under its
protection into larger, hopefully more viable political units
that would be granted independence. This was the model
for Malaya (the Malay sultanates), the Trucial Coast (the
sultanates of the Persian Gulf), and southern Arabia. British
protectorates there had been patched up in 1962 into two

larger units: a "Federation of South Arabia" (South Yemen) and a "Protectorate of South Arabia" (Hadramawt). Independence was promised to both for 1968, but rather than a dignified affair, Britain's departure from Aden would be somewhat expeditious and disorderly.

The cause for urgency was a couple of insurgent groups with Marxist and Nasserist inclinations, active in the hills around Aden: the Front for the Liberation of Occupied South Yemen and the more redoubtable National Liberation Front. The National Liberation Front had a hegemonic bent: by November 1967, as the British departed, it had succeeded in imposing its authority over its rival and proclaimed a People's Republic of South Yemen, which unified all the former British protectorates (both South Yemen and the Hadramawt). Its leaders talked about "scientific socialism" as a developmental project, echoing Barre's program for Somalia. Following an internal coup in 1970 by Marxist hard-liners, the country was renamed People's Democratic Republic of Yemen, to better signal the alignment with Moscow and the ambitions toward North Yemen. In 1978, as the regime adopted single-party rule, the Front would change its name to the Yemeni Socialist Party.

The northern Arab republic responded favorably to the idea of unification with the southern Democratic Republic, which was programmatically announced by Yemeni leaders from both sides in 1972. It is hard to imagine how the fact that one state was under the watch of Saudi Arabia and the other a protégé of the Soviet Union could have been surmounted. But in the 1970s, there were still enough Pan-Arabist sentiments going around to make that kind of talk politically valuable. The first president of North Yemen, Abdul Rahman al-Iryani, was a conciliatory figure who seemed to believe that Yemeni nationalism would trump ideological divisions and keep foreign influences at bay. In any case, the unification moment of the early 1970s may have remained purely declaratory, but it laid the foundations for a process that would take under different leaders, under different circumstances.

In the early years of the northern republic, the strongman behind the regime was Ibrahim al-Hamdi, a military officer and a modernist with ambitions to take down the tribes. Al-Hamdi seized power from al-Iryani in a 1974 palace coup. He immediately set out on a program of modernization and development of state capacity at the expense of rural, tribal power bases. He, too, went along with the idea of a union with the south. The north had a much larger population, oil reserves had been identified in the south, and Aden's connection with the Soviet Union held promises of economic development and of centralization of authority in a stronger state. His efforts were understandably resisted by the tribes. In 1977, tribal elements working as agents of Saudi Arabia got to him: his body was found riddled with bullets in the company of murdered prostitutes. Riyadh would not have a strong republican regime in Sanaa, especially one that flirted with socialists.

The Zaidi Mutawakkilite Kingdom had handled centrifugal tribal forces with medieval methods. The families of tribal chiefs were held hostage in the royal palace, and the lands of troublemakers were seized and redistributed to more loyal vassals. Given the lack of sustained economic growth, it was a form of dynamic stasis based on the divide-and-rule strategy that lasted until the 1962 coup. The successors of the imams, the leaders of the republican regime, would use a similar methodology augmented by public expenditures. Revenue in the 1970s came mostly from import taxes and foreign aid: it was not much to go by, but social expectations were not high. In 1975, the population in the north was under 5 million, with more than half under the age of 16 and with almost 100% female illiteracy.

Patronage and the enduring strength of the tribal structure in the north helped stabilize the regime after 1970. The question of leadership was settled when Ali Abdullah Saleh, an officer with limited education but decent connections and exceptional skills at manipulation, became president of the republic in 1978, following the murders in quick succession of two of his predecessors. Saleh would keep the flirtation with the Soviet Union in the 1980s with a treaty of friendship. However, keen to retain Saudi aid, he kept the northern republic on a nonaligned course. Saleh was no visionary reformist but a manipulator who settled in for the long haul. Of Zaidi origins, he was from the Sanhan tribe, a village branch of the Hashid confederation, second only in numbers to the Bakil confederation. The Hashids were led by Shaykh Abdullah al-Ahmar, a powerful figure who, until his death in 2007, would play a constructive if often oppositional role in the political life of the new regime.

It was an odd arrangement, institutionally speaking, but this balance of power between Saleh and al-Ahmar brought the tribal structure into the fold of the northern republic. Patronage flowed along patron-client lines, buying loyalty to the status quo. For those at the bottom of the social ladder, left out from the spoils, there was always emigration to the wealthier Saudi Arabia and to the Gulf. Yemen, north and south, has been a net exporter of mostly unskilled labor throughout the decades that followed independence. For the north, remittances in the 1970s were the main source of foreign reserves, sufficient to generate a current account surplus.

The two Yemens had an agricultural economic base—with khat, a narcotic, an important staple. In the 1960s, oil reserves were found in the eastern Shabwah province, at the time part of the Marxist south. Production would not begin in earnest until the mid-1980s. Another field in Ma'rib province would not be exploited until the 1990s. In the 1970s, the potential for revenues from oil seemed to stack the deck in favor of Aden, which had a small population under 2 million. Yet the Marxist south found it difficult to stabilize. Perhaps it was excess of ambition that doomed it. Attempts at state-led industrialization never really took off. Meanwhile, with the backing of the Soviet Union, the restless ideologues in Aden got caught up in troubles with their neighbors. In the east, they supported a Marxist insurgency in Dhofar against the sultan of Oman. In the conservative, Zaidi-dominated north, they stirred unrest among leftist and Sunni groups, bringing the two Yemens to the edge of war over a 1979 border incident. All the while, Aden failed to resolve its internal power struggles. The leadership of the Yemen Socialist Party was agitated by coups and counter-coups from the mid-1980s—a situation in which Saudi Arabia is suspected to have had a hand, as it strived to undermine the socialist regime.

And so a fragile south found itself exposed when the Soviet Union withdrew from world affairs in 1989. The end of the Cold War forced open a window of opportunity for negotiations about reunification to resume, an attractive prospect for the north given that oil revenues from the southern fields had started to come in. The united Republic of Yemen that saw the day in May 1990 was meant to be a merger of equals, with Saleh in the presidential seat and Ali Salim al-Baidh, the southern socialist leader, serving as vice president. The head of government, Haidar Abu Bakr al-Attas, was another socialist from the south, where he had previously occupied the same position. The capital was the northern political capital of Sanaa, with the seaport of Aden the natural economic center of the unified country. The process of unification, in the international limelight, was pledged to the creation of a modern, democratic constitution, guaranteeing property rights and free elections.

The unified republic was rapidly tested by the influx of Yemeni workers—in the hundreds of thousands—expelled from Saudi Arabia and the Gulf states in retaliation for their government's professed "neutrality" in relation to the August 1990 Iraqi conquest of Kuwait. Riyadh had always been wary of the Yemens, the north because it was republican and the south because it was socialist. The northern

Yemen Arab Republic, although protected by Riyadh, had never been allowed in the Gulf Cooperation Council—the exclusive club of conservative emirs and kings of the Arabian Peninsula. Saudi suspicions were confirmed by President Saleh's betrayal. Like King Hussein of Jordan, another beneficiary of Saudi largesse, the Yemeni leader had cast his lot with Saddam Hussein's assault on the regional order.

The lack of jobs and resources to care for the returnees created a social crisis, coincident with a political crisis caused by the unworkable arrangements of a constitution that shared responsibilities between northern and southern leaders. The 1993 elections were unfavorable to the Yemeni Socialist Party, and tension grew between the partners as the southerners felt marginalized. It quickly reached a point where Aden seceded, in May 1994. Saudi Arabia, still resentful of the betrayal in the summer of 1990, was converted to the merits of divide and rule and provided covert support to the southern forces. Unification was recent, military forces had not yet been integrated, and a separation seemed attainable. But the northern army rolled in, making short work of the southern secessionists. It was all settled by July. The constitution was simplified, giving more power to the president, and while the Yemen Socialist Party remained, it had lost its bite. It was all settled by July. The constitution was simplified, giving more power to the president, and while the Yemen Socialist Party remained, it had lost its bite. The new player was Al-Islah, the party dominated by Shaykh Abdullah al-Ahmar, which somehow managed the feat of bringing together the Hashid tribal confederation of which he was the supreme shaykh, the local section of the Muslim Brotherhood, and the salafis led by the radical Shaykh Abdul Majeed al-Zindani. Al-Zindani was an odd figure, the founder of an Iman University in Sanaa whose students allegedly killed Christian missionaries and a prominent socialist leader. Like other scholars associated with the Muslim Brotherhood and da'awa movement, Al-Zindani had maintained over the years relationships with organizations and charities in Saudi Arabia. He had organized in Yemen an Assembly for the Propagation of Virtue and Prohibition of Vice, a vigilante version of the Saudi religious police. The religious terrain in Yemen was somewhat favorable to men like Al-Zindani. While attitudes toward religion tend to be folkish rather than scripturally fundamentalist—if anything because illiteracy is high—there is a poor and undereducated segment of society from which come stories such as that of Arwa, a nine-year-old girl who, in 2008, went to court on her own initiative to ask for a divorce from a man who had bought her from her parents. Al-Zindani's religious committee was on the side of the husband, but the judge was not, and granted her a divorce while the government contemplated imposing a minimal age of consent.

What brought together an old warrior like Al-Ahmar and a lunatic like Al-Zindani was their common opposition to the godless Yemen Socialist Party. In the name of ideology, Sunni Islamist militants and former mujahideen—veterans from the Afghan jihad against the Soviets—had fought on the side of the north during the 1994 civil war. The Saudis may have preferred had Saleh lost that war, but they made the best of it by leveraging Islam and hard cash to keep him in check. Yemen is said to have received $2 billion in Saudi aid every year following the civil war, and at the same time Yemeni Imams were given Saudi scholarships to study abroad, and local da'awa organizations were the beneficiaries of donations. Patronage allowed Riyadh to influence social and political attitudes in the neighboring republic, and the people of the south, who had for decades lived a relatively secular life, first under British rule, then under a Marxist regime, were becoming visibly more religious.

Saleh was at ease with the activities of the salafis, as they helped him to colonize the south. Islamists had vested interests in the survival of his regime. Politically, Al-Islah, the Islamist party, acted as a conservative but loyal opposition to the regime. Al-Islah was the main alternative to the president's General People's Congress, and whether in or out of the government, it gave Yemen a veneer of democratic life and kept the Saudis in the game.

This state of affairs could have gone on, if not for the fact that the population expanded tremendously and oil revenue did not. Growing at 2.7 percent a year, Yemen's population neared 24 million in 2010, half under the age of 18 and two-thirds under 23. At the time, the unemployment and illiteracy rates were in the 40 percent range, and 40 percent of the population subsisted on less than $2 a day. Yemen's weak tax base was unable to support the policy of subsidies and patronage on a sufficient scale. Rent-seeking as a developmental model is a zero-sum game bound to test the ability of any regime to redistribute finite resources. When there is no growth per capita, people get jealous. Rural tribes that felt neglected by the government came into the habit of abducting foreign tourists, released in exchange for infrastructure investments. Over time, the entourage of President Saleh appeared more greedy, corrupt, clannish, delegitimizing the delicate system.

The Saudis, who have since the 1960s been on the front line of the ups and downs of the Yemeni state, bear no illusions about the condition of their neighbor. During a meeting with U.S. envoy Richard Holbrooke in May 2009, Prince Mohammed bin Nayef, the son of the Interior minister and also the No. 2 in the ministry, described Yemen as an "extremely dangerous . . . failed state" where the power of the president is restricted to Sanaa, the capital. In the course of that conversation, the prince deplored the level of corruption, lamenting that money transfers from Saudi Arabia ended up in Swiss bank accounts.

Yemen's reputation for corruption deterred foreign investments. An independent Supreme National Authority for Combating Corruption was established in 2007 to seduce potential investors by investigating and exposing corruption. The agency, a partnership between the public and private sectors, remained mostly quiet until November 2010, when 117 public officials, five of whom were governors and ambassadors, were spectacularly referred for prosecution to the judicial authorities, as the leadership of the agency toured the world capitals to advertise its progress. It was urgent: Riyadh had resorted to bypassing the government and working directly with the tribes. The Saudis were hoping that direct investment in rural areas would assure them the enduring loyalty of the tribes, independently of the fate of the regime in Sanaa.

Matters had come to grief in 2004, when a Zaidi religious leader, Shaykh Hussein Badreddin al-Houthi, was killed by government forces. Al-Houthi had assembled in Sa'ada—the historical heartland of the Zaidi imamate—a youth group under the name of Al-Shabab al Mu'minin (the Young Believers). Al-Houthi aimed to reinvigorate the Zaidi faith under pressure from the Sunni salafis then proselytizing in northern Yemen. Fundamentalism allowed Saleh to anchor the south, but the presence and growing visibility of salafis in the north was perceived as a threat by the Zaidi elite, which triggered a bout of civil war.

The Houthi phenomenon was not strictly about religion. The group that formed around Shaykh al-Houthi and became known as "the Houthis" drew support from well-armed Zaidi tribal elements alienated by the regime for financial reasons. The faith-based movement had morphed into a tribal militia that clashed with the Yemeni Army in the summer of 2004. Shaykh al-Houthi was killed in the months that followed that first confrontation, and his death catalyzed the movement as his father and brothers took over leadership roles. Violence escalated, alternating between phases of open conflict and fragile truces, with each new outbreak more threatening for the regime. Saudi Arabia got involved in late 2009. The Houthis had fallen back to take positions in Saudi territory, where about 1 million Zaidis live. Despite its reservations toward—and its contempt for—the Yemeni government, Riyadh felt compelled to crush a rebellion at its border of what Prince

Mohammed bin Nayef described as a band of Shia *takfiris* ("apostates"). There are reports that artillery was used, and even of air strikes targeting the Houthis' positions.

Victims of what is known as the Houthi Rebellion or the Sa'ada Insurgency can be counted in the thousands, with hundreds of thousands internally displaced persons. The numbers are uncertain, as NGOs and journalists were not allowed in the area. The conflict has been fogged up by dubious claims aimed at delegitimizing one party or the other, in particular regarding the roles of Iran, Al Qaeda, and the United States in the unfolding of events. The only certainty is that the conflict marked a loss of support for Saleh's government from a substantial segment of the Zaidi tribal base. Saudi Arabia's intervention is also well ascertained—an extraordinary move from a country whose armed forces had not seen combat operations since the 1960s, when elements of the Saudi National Guard were fighting Egyptian forces alongside the Zaidi royalists. Both parties have sought to drag the United States to its side, or at least to neutralize it: the Houthis in the name of human rights and democracy, the regime in the name of law and order. In this game, the government of Yemen has been advantaged because it could play the Al Qaeda card, a priority for Washington.

By 2010, Yemen was failing as a state. Oil reserves were expected to last no more than another decade and with them would go the rent that kept the country together. The only plan for the post-oil era was new reserves of natural gas—a hydrocarbon miracle following another. Yemen LNG, a joint venture with French petroleum giant Total

that started production in 2009, was hoped to be a lifeline
to future foreign currency. Water resources had been poorly
managed, leading to shortages that were bound to get worse
with a growing population. The water problem was in part
of Yemen's own making, as a better state would have ration-
alized the use of water and arable land on the eastern plateaus. But there is often negative feedback at play among
lack of state capacity, insecurity, and underdevelopment.
The oil rent had discouraged productive activity, allowing
to import most goods. Agriculture, the economic basis of
the country, had shifted from subsistence staples to the cultivation of water-intensive khat. As diverse and venerated
as wine, khat is a cultural phenomenon: the variety of the
bush, the soil on which it is grown, the color and texture of
leaves are recognized to participate to the unique signature
of each "vintage." But for all the poetry of khat, the plant
takes a heavy toll on limited aquifers, not to mention on
the consumers' quality of life as the habit can consume 30%
of their income and occupy a third of their day. Various
reports estimate the contribution of khat to Yemen's GDP
to be well over 10%, and its cultivation is said to employ a
third of the agricultural labor force. Since 2008, the World-
bank has been working with the government on a crop
replacement program still in its infancy.

In predominantly rural Yemen, the patronage system had
maintained the tribal structure, and it is from the tribal
structure that protests came as the limits of patronage were
being tested. As the government was forced to pick and
choose its favorite beneficiaries, those being left in the cold
were tempted to go their own way. The Houthi Rebellion

crystallized the discontent within the Zaidi north. Similar developments occurred from around 2007 in the Shafi'i south, where an incipient Southern Movement renewed the demands to secede from a unified Yemen. The secessionists were a loose alliance of tribal chiefs in low-density, rural areas, limited in numbers and capability. They mostly engaged in peaceful protests in the countryside, but there have been more serious incidents, with exchanges of gunfire with government troops, and ambushes in which government officials have been killed.

In April 2009, the Southern Movement got a boost when Tariq al-Fadhli, an erstwhile ally of President Saleh, came out in support and established himself as a leading figure for the secession. Al-Fadhli has an interesting pedigree. From the tribal elite in the province of Abyan, east of Aden, he is the scion of a family dispossessed by the socialist regime. He grew up in exile, in Saudi Arabia, and from there left for Afghanistan in the 1980s to fight the Soviets. Returning in the early 1990s, he was mentioned in connection with a 1992 terrorist attack against American soldiers in transit through Aden. When the civil war erupted in 1994, Al-Fadhli led his mujahideen on the side of the north against the atheist south. For years after that, he would remain under the fold of President Saleh, a man of the regime until his about-face in 2009. Like others in the secessionist movement, Al-Fadhli seeks to distinguish his action from that of the global jihadists of Al Qaeda. Their goal is not to wage war on the West, but to re-create an independent south that they felt has been annexed and plundered by Sanaa. Al-Fadhli has acknowledged his history as a mujahideen and his position as a spokesman for the Yemeni mujahideen. But to make the point that he did not harbor ill will toward the United States, he went as far as raising the American flag in front of his compound.

In addition to the Houthi Rebellion and the Southern Movement, Yemen is host to a group of jihadists that calls itself Al Qaeda in the Arabian Peninsula, the subject of a subsequent chapter. "Balkanization" became a word in 1919. Its more recent Arabic equivalent is *Sawmala*, the risk of "Somalization" Yemen faces by having to fight on three fronts. But the luck of Saleh's regime was that its opponents were divided in their identity and objectives, and that each operated in its own sphere, both ideological and geographical. Saleh's tenure in power had been long, even by Middle East standards. It was believed that he had in mind bequeathing power to his eldest son, Ahmed, who strategically headed the Presidential Guard and Special Forces. This unpopular dynastic prospect had eventually brought together the Islamist Al-Islah and the Yemeni Socialist Party in a "Joint Meeting Parties," in order to field a common candidate in the 2006 presidential elections. The effort was to no avail: Saleh was reelected and looked set to complete his final term running until 2013.

Then came the Tunisian revolution of January 2011. The self-immolation of a street vendor in a remote Tunisian town inspired similar gestures of protest in Yemen, already in the midst of an economic, social, and political crisis. By the end of the month, tens of thousands of Yemenis were in the streets of the main cities, rallying around a pink banner, calling for Saleh's resignation. The picture was not uniform. In the south, in Aden, protests were unruly and demands radical. In Sanaa, protests remained, at first, a contained, civilized affair. Students and protesters occupied the area around Sanaa University, demanding economic opportunities, greater access for women to education, and an accountable government preferably without the current president. But the parallel demonstrations organized by the traditional opposition, united under the banner of the "Joint Meeting Parties," were orderly. There was Al-Islah, the socialists and smaller opposition parties, along with civil society associations such as the National Organization for Defending Rights and Freedom, and the Yemeni Journalists Syndicates. They would have welcomed a change at the helm of the republic but seemed content with reforms. Saleh benefited from the benign attitude he—unlike his Tunisian counterpart—had had for decades toward Islamists. Al-Islah, the principal opposition party, had vested interest in the system and was paying the president back in kind with limited demands.

The wily ruler moved quickly to disarm the crisis. He announced that he would not seek reelection after 2013—a promise he had made and broken during each previous election—and more importantly that his son Ahmed, notorious for corruption, would not run either. He took a spate of precautionary measures: raising salaries of the military, imposing price controls, reducing taxes. With his sons, nephews and Sanhan tribesmen well-established in the military and security apparatus, it seemed there was little chance of a coup. Saleh owed his decades in power to his ability to coopt and balance tribal and party leaders, with no regard for the long-term fiscal and economic viability of his country. Throwing money at the problem and promising political and financial concessions could work once again.

But this time the people had a mind of their own, and the protests showed that tribal and party alignments had their limits. As contagion spread to the rest of the region, as one autocratic regime after another stumbled or fell, the Yemeni president appeared vulnerable. By late February, protests had become massive in Sanaa as well as Aden, and spread to other cities. They were led by youth groups outside of the traditional political arrangements, a popular wave that tribal and opposition leaders eventually decided to ride. Shaykh Abdullah al-Ahmar had for many years been the Speaker of the Parliament and the powerful leader of Al-Islah and of the Hashid tribal confederation. After he had passed away in 2007, his sons had risen to prominence. The elder, Sadiq, had taken over his father's mantle as the main figure of a loyal opposition, while the younger Hussein al-Ahmar had done the President's bidding, negotiating on his behalf the ceasefire with the Houthis. In late February 2011, the al-Ahmar brothers and a few prominent leaders of the Bakil confederation joined the crowds demanding Saleh's resignation. Tribal defections were not yet universal but opportunistic, revealing that Shaykhs had already begun competing within themselves for the spoils of the dying regime.

The al-Ahmars were a powerful clan, but they could not claim to unify the protesters and there was no clear path for a post-Saleh political order. The president spared no effort to keep his position, gutting the constitution to rebalance power from the presidency to the parliament, and dismissing his cabinet. But crowds of young men and women, side by side, kept rejecting any arrangement. Protests grew in intensity throughout March, each Friday bringing new waves of demonstrators in all the main cities. On March 18th, the leader lost his nerves and snipers shot at the crowd, killing over 50. The bloodshed prompted the defection of Brigadier General Ali Mohsen al-Ahmar (unrelated to the al-Ahmars), the powerful commander of the 1st Armored Division. His troops established a security perimeter around Sanaa University to protect the protesters, occasionally clashing with elements loyal to the president. It was an incestuous affair, Ali Mohsen being a relative of the president, as were the main commanders in the loyalist camp.

On April 12th, more bloodshed of civilian protesters in the city of Taiz drove Western capitals to finally come out and request Saleh's resignation. The president had finally unified most factions against him, and the international community as well. In the coalition that demanded a regime change were the traditional electoral opposition in the Joint Meeting Parties (the Islamists of Al-Islah, the socialists), the secessionist Southern Movement (who had for now suspended demands for secession), the Zaidi Houthis (who demanded regional autonomy), the mass of young protesters and the army defectors. While the United

States took a backseat in the ensuing negotiations, the Gulf
Cooperation Council, led by Saudi Arabia with Qatar in its
wings, proposed an exit strategy to the embattled leader.
Executive powers would be temporarily transferred to the
Vice-President, and the opposition would form a transi-
tional government.

The young protestors wished for a great purge akin to
what was happening at the same time in Tunisia and Egypt,
where former elites were brought to trial and the ruling parties were dissolved. But the Yemeni ruling party, the General People Congress, retained enough of a power base to
expect a central role in the post-Saleh era, and it demanded
an orderly transition of power with guarantees for the
future. That was the idea behind the Saudi plan, and the
political opposition of the Joint Meeting Parties was
inclined to acquiesce. Unlike Tunisia and Egypt, each ruled
by a single-party in an authoritarian fashion, Yemen had
experienced under Saleh a skewed form of democracy,
where elections had been relatively free and the political
parties and tribal elites had conspired together to divide the
spoils of oil sales.

Saleh stalled to negotiate immunity from prosecution for
himself and his kin. And when he got those concessions
from the Joint Meeting Parties, against the wishes of the
street protesters, he accepted on three different occasions to
resign, and each time reneged at the last minute, causing
attending Arab and Western diplomats to lose face. There
was the matter of the deceptive character of the president,
and also his wild hope that if he could hold on to power

long enough, he might live to see the heterogeneous alliance fracture. He still had the backing of the units commanded by his son and nephews, who were brought in from the south at the end of May. A violent crackdown in restive Taiz was followed by a showdown in Sanaa between loyalists and the tribal militias assembled around the compound of the al-Ahmars.

It was, finally, a civil war, and it did not go well for Saleh. Not only did the al-Ahmars hold their ground in their Sanaa neighborhood, but also they succeeded at getting at Saleh who was severely burned, along with several members of his cabinet, in an explosion in the palace mosque during the Friday payers of June 3rd. The Saudis jumped on the opportunity to whisk him out of the country for medical care, but it was too late for an orderly transition. Armed units were facing each other in the capital, and the provinces, north and south, were in a state of utter confusion as Houthi and salafi militias had taken over towns abandoned by the regular army. It looked as if entire provinces had passed beyond the control of the government. The Houthis were running the show in the northern province of Sa'ada. As for the south, the secessionists and the salafists were taking their chances in the political vacuum Saleh had created.

CHAPTER FOUR

In the Land of the Mahdi: Sudan

SUDAN'S HISTORY is as checkered as that of its neighbors, with a colonial period ending with some patch-up job at independence, a dystopic democracy, long spells of military dictatorship, and civil wars verging on genocide. The greatest source of tension has been between a Semitic, Muslim north—the alluvial plateau where the Blue and White Niles merge near Khartoum—and a Nilotic, non-Muslim, south—the marshy lands of the Dinkas and the Nuers, favorite subjects of cultural anthropologists. Britain had administered both regions independently of each other—if anything, to prevent the spread of malaria from the southern swamps to the northern plain—but had nonetheless forced the south under the sovereignty of Khartoum at the time of independence, in 1956. The graft never took and ended in 2011, following a widely approved referendum over the question of secession forced by a half-century of conflict.

Islam has played an important place in the country's recent history, if anything because of the role of Mahdi

Muhammad Ahmad as the foundational nationalist hero of modern Sudan. In the twentieth century, an active political faction, the Ummah Party, formed around his legacy. The leadership of the Ummah Party fell to Sadiq al-Mahdi, born in 1935, a man of great elegance and royal demeanor. He also was the imam of Al-Ansar, the religious group founded by his great-grandfather, Muhammad Ahmad. Another Islamist party, the Democratic Unionist Party, has its roots in the Khatmiyah Sufi order, which was in the nineteenth century a rival to Al-Ansar. The third pillar of postindependence political Islam in Sudan has been the local offshoot of the Muslim Brotherhood, most commonly known as the National Islamic Front, and led by Hassan al-Turabi. Al-Turabi, born in 1932, was formerly the dean of the School of Law at the University of Khartoum, and is the brother-in-law of Sadiq al-Mahdi.

Islamic parties have been in and out of government since independence. In the 1970s, many a military leader—in Pakistan, in Egypt—has used Islamists against liberal or communist circles to bolster their autocratic rule. In Sudan, this was the case with Jafaar al-Numayri, a "free officer" who came to power in a 1969 coup. The vicissitudes of his tenure at the helm of the state were dominated by failed attempts to resolve the secessionist struggle in the south, which compelled him to rely increasingly on the Islamists. Al-Numayri is remembered for instituting Shariah as law of the land in September 1983, in an attempt to placate the opposition to his unpopular rule. That did not save him; he was overthrown in 1985. Sadiq al-Mahdi took over the reins of a coalition government dominated by the three Islamist parties before another officer, Omar al-Bashir, seized power in a 1989 coup. Al-Bashir prudently abolished the position of prime minister but he, too, needed support from Islamists. While Sadiq al-Mahdi was placed under house arrest, Al-Turabi and his acolytes were retained in the government. Al-Turabi had studied law in London and Paris, and was an expert in Islamic law as applied (in theory) to the governance of a modern state. The Bashir regime was the occasion for him to test his ideas about an Islamic state in the political reality of Sudan—which was, in essence, an Islamized version of an African strongman regime. Beyond domestic politics, Al-Turabi and the National Islamic Front had an ambitious foreign policy agenda. For one, they aspired to federate various Muslim revolutionary groups and radicals in a sort of International Islamist Association. To that purpose, Khartoum hosted a Popular Arab Islamic Conference in 1991, 1993, and 1995, designed as an antithesis to the state-based Organization of the Islamic Conference and Arab League, which were dominated by Saudi Arabia and Egypt.

Islamists of all flavors are said to have come for those occasions: mujahideen such as Osama bin Laden and Ayman al-Zawahiri, Palestinians including members of the Abu Nidal Organization, members of Hezbollah, and representatives of the Iranian Revolutionary Guards, among others. Al-Turabi and his followers had no animus toward the Shia; on the contrary, the hope was to bring all Muslims together on a common anti-imperialist stance, crystallized around the issue of the liberation of Palestine. Their success in achieving that federative goal seems limited, and claims that everyone who was anyone in the Islamist terrorist underground was in Khartoum in the early 1990s remain dubious. Imad Mughniyeh, the master terrorist operative of Hezbollah, may or may not have met Osama bin Laden in Khartoum in June 1994. In any case, the consequences of such meetings, to the extent that they took place, were minimal. The jihadist "federation" remained a chimera, like the fanciful notion of reforming an Islamic caliphate.

In the early 1990s, Khartoum was simply a haven for militants who had survived the turbulent era of the Cold War and found themselves with nowhere else to go. That was the case of "Carlos," a Venezuelan-born terrorist who had peaked in the 1970s, and had recently fallen out with his Syrian patrons. That was also the case of Arab mujahideen, veterans of the war against the Soviet Union in Afghanistan. In 1992, with the Russians out of Central Asia, the glorious jihad was over and Pakistan no longer welcomed foreign mujahideen in the region. The so-called Arab-Afghans had no home to go back to; they were drifters at war with their government, brought together by both ideology and necessity, looking for a new sanctuary or a new cause. Bosnia would open a battlefield for some of them, with the tacit agreement of the Saudi state and the resources of the old support network. Others would find their war in Chechnya. Others still would participate in the short-lived Yemeni civil war, in 1994.

Sudan offered a place of exile to the Arab-Afghan mujahideen. Exile was the fate of Saudi-born Osama bin Laden, a moneyman for the jihad. He had barely returned a hero in his native Saudi Arabia, in 1990, before he was banished for his vocal criticism of the Saudi monarch's decision to allow American troops on sacred land to hold off an expansionist Saddam Hussein. In return for a safe haven in Sudan, Bin Laden had arranged for financial investments in the local infrastructure. There, with him, was a strong contingent of Egyptians on the run from their government. As a place of exile, Khartoum was the closest to Cairo, the great Arab capital that lured farther down the Nile.

Sudan and Egypt have had an intimate and acrimonious history, with Cairo often looking down on Khartoum as its possession, as a land of inferiors in need of guidance. The Egyptian veterans of the Afghan jihad who gathered in the Sudanese capital in the early 1990s were affiliated with a radical splinter of the Egyptian Muslim Brotherhood known as Tanzim al-Jihad, or "Islamic Jihad." The jihad group shared a pedigree with a sister movement: Gama'at Islamiyah. Both were radical offshoots of the Muslim Brotherhood, and both embraced armed struggle as a primary political tool. But where Gama'at Islamiyah was a broad, clandestine organization, well established in Upper Egypt and in the shantytowns of Cairo, the jihad group was a small faction of Afghan veterans at the margins of the main conflict then playing out on Egyptian soil. Most were of middle-class origins, urban and well-educated. They were not the rural riffraff who composed the rank and file of Gama'at, and bullied the Copts of Upper Egypt.

Violence flared between Gama'at and the Egyptian order in the late 1980s, and by 1992–93 it had escalated to insurgency levels in parts of the country, a civil war that would run its course for the better part of the decade. The much smaller jihad group had a few operational assets in Cairo, but its leadership was either in prison or in exile. There was Abud al-Zumur, an Egyptian lieutenant colonel and the highest-ranking officer implicated in the assassination of President Anwar Sadat, imprisoned since 1981. There was Sayyed Imam al-Sharif, better known as Dr. Fadl, who had spent the late 1980s in Pakistan, coordinating with Egyptian mujahideen. There was Ayman al-Zawahiri, another medical doctor, arrested and tortured in the roundup following the assassination of Sadat, who had moved to Pakistan upon his release from prison. Finally there was Omar Abdel Rahman, the blind Egyptian cleric who, after a similar spell in Egyptian prisons in the early 1980s, had also moved to Peshawar during the jihad. More than a cadre, Abdel Rahman was a spiritual figure for all Egyptian jihadists. Born in 1938, he had twenty years over the older mujahideen, born in the 1950s. In the early 1990s, he resettled in Jersey City, New Jersey, as the imam of a local mosque.

It is within Rahman's entourage that the FBI would find the operatives involved in the first attack against New York's World Trade Center, in February 1993. The bombing was the overture to a "day of terror," an operation in the planning stages involving simultaneous attacks against bridges, tunnels, and other symbolic landmarks of the American financial and cultural capital. The motives claimed for the operations centered on the issue of American support to Israel—a virulently Zionist rabbi had recently been killed in New York by the same lot. The men captured in relation to the World Trade Center attack included an Egyptian (Mahmud Abouhalima), a Sudanese (Siddiq Ibrahim Siddiq 'Ali), and other Arabs. The strategic thinking behind the decision to attack the United States in 1993 needs consideration. Palestinian groups have by and large stayed away from American targets, even when the United States was most indifferent to the plight of the Palestinian people. Not even Hamas deviates from this basic cautionary principle. In its early years, Lebanese Hezbollah had attacked American targets in Beirut, but it, too, quickly restrained its behavior. The sudden attempt by the Egyptians and their associates to take down one of Manhattan's landmarks was a radical departure from established patterns. It could have been the issue of American support for the Mubarak regime at a time when violence was reaching a state of paroxysm in Cairo. Or it could have been a piece in a puzzle that was already well beyond the issues of Egypt and Israel.

The planners of the 1993 attack were the remarkable pair of Khalid Sheikh Mohammed and nephew Ramzi Yousef, Balochis born in Kuwait and educated in the West. Khalid Sheikh Mohammed's signature—spectacular, simultaneous attacks against American or Western targets—would be apparent in all the significant operations of Al Qaeda, from its beginnings in the early 1990s to 2002, when the U.S.-led invasion of Afghanistan put an end to it. The decision to attack American targets seems to date from 1991–92, a time when Al Qaeda barely existed as an organization, let alone as a brand name. The Afghan jihad had grown sour grapes:

witness the gesture of Mir Aimal Kasi, a Pakistani from Quetta who, in January 1993, self-inspired, gunned down passengers in cars waiting at a red light to enter the CIA headquarters in Langley, Virginia.

Osama bin Laden had arrived in Sudan in 1991; he was in Khartoum when mujahideen first attacked American targets in Aden, on December 29, 1992. The bombs were set off in the Movenpick and Gold Mohur luxury hotels where American soldiers were (incorrectly) thought to be billeted on their way to the ill-fated relief mission in Somalia. Among the suspects were locals Jamal al-Nahdi and Tariq al-Fadhli—the same Tariq al-Fadhli from Abyan, who years later would lead the secessionist Southern Movement. At the time, Al-Fadhli had just returned from Afghanistan. He apparently had crossed paths there with Osama bin Laden, and the name of the Saudi was also mentioned in the postmortem of the attack. Two months after the Aden operation, a truck bomb exploded in the basement garage of New York's World Trade Center.

The journey of Osama bin Laden has been retraced in many accounts, his connections explored. There was his relationship with Prince Turki al-Faisal, the head of Saudi intelligence, which dated from the Afghan jihad. It is futile to speculate on the exact nature and extent of the bond between the two men, and between the Saudi adventurer and the government of his country. In any case, a strong signal was sent in April 1994, when Bin Laden's citizenship was publicly revoked. Not all his contacts may have gone that way. Prince Zayed bin Sultan of Abu Dhabi could have remained a patron to the Saudi far into the 1990s, a possible source for the money with which Bin Laden paid his hosts, first in Sudan and later in Afghanistan. The Saudi would visit the Afghan hunting camps of emirati princes until 1999, once allegedly meeting Sheikh Mohammed bin Rashid al-Maktoum, the future emir of Dubai.

In 1990, following upon the success in Afghanistan against the Soviet Union, it would have been natural for the mujahideen to set their sights on the liberation of Palestine, the cause célèbre of Muslim disenfranchisement. This was the position of Abdullah Azzam, the most eminent of the so-called Arab-Afghans, and a Palestinian. But Azzam was mysteriously killed in late 1989, and the mujahideen would never go anywhere near Palestine. Arguing at the time in a seminal article that "the road to al-Quds [Jerusalem] went through Cairo," Al-Zawahiri had proposed that the mujahideen target instead the "near enemy," the Mubarak regime that had tortured him. This was a traditional position for the Egyptians, an argument already made in the 1970s by Muhammed Abd al-Salam Faraj, an electrical engineer and Islamist ideologue, the founder of the jihad group, who had called for the assassination of President Sadat.

The third option was to look beyond Palestine and the Arab regimes. The attacks of 1992 in Aden shed some light on the attack of 1993 in New York. It is possible that the United States was not a secondary target for the jihadists, a target of opportunity after the battle had been lost on the home turf, as is generally argued. In the early 1990s, when bombs were going off in Aden and New York, Khalid

Sheikh Mohammed and nephew Ramzi Yousef were in the Philippines plotting to take down multiple American airliners in flight and to assassinate the pope, the president of the Philippines, and U.S. President Clinton. This was not about Israel. This was not about Mubarak and the Arab regimes complacent toward Israel. This was about America and the West. The Egyptians would come to that opinion as well, but only later, after the failure of the Islamic revolution in Egypt had been consummated.

The structure of the jihad group was compromised by a severe security failure: at some point between late 1992 and early 1993, depending on the accounts, Egyptian security had gotten its hands on a hard drive with a list of members. When the jihad group attempted to kill the Egyptian prime minister with a car bomb in November 1993, Cairo members were swiftly rounded up and jailed. The group was brought to its knees, its leaders cut off from Egypt, and forced to take a hard look at a new strategy, a reflection that tore the exiles apart. Dr. Fadl, a respected mujahideen and founding member of the Al Qaeda *shura* (the council of leaders), had joined his peers in Sudan earlier in the year. In 1994, taking stock of the situation, he cut all ties with the militants and moved to Yemen, devoting himself to the practice of field medicine. That same year, a dejected Al-Zawahiri moved to Bulgaria, making himself useful by coordinating international support to foreign mujahideen in nearby Bosnia. He would remain there until the end of that war. In December 1996, he was arrested in Dagestan while attempting to cross into Chechnya, and was briefly detained.

Their Egyptian acolytes who remained in Sudan adapted to the situation and fell back on a transnational strategy that was in line with the global orientation of the nascent Al Qaeda. Egyptian jihadists would conduct two significant operations in 1995. The first occurred in June, when the motorcade of President Hosni Mubarak was attacked during an African Union summit in Addis Ababa. The second took place in November, when seventeen people were killed in the Egyptian Embassy in Islamabad in a raid by commandos armed with guns, grenades, and car bombs. Ethiopia was chosen because it was close to Sudan and offered a unique chance to get at Mubarak. Pakistan was chosen because the Arab mujahideen kept connections there from the time of the Afghan War. They resented the ongoing cooperation between Pakistani and Egyptian governments in deporting mujahideen back to Cairo. Hounded in their home country, those men had traveled to south Asia in the 1980s to fight Pakistan's war. Now that the war was won and they were no longer wanted, they were turned over to a government that routinely tortured them during interrogation. The CIA was allegedly involved in that early incarnation of the rendition program.

It was the attack in the Ethiopian capital against Mubarak that had the strongest impact, even though it missed its target. Cairo denounced as the mastermind of the attack Mustafa Hamza, the leader of the paramilitary branch of Gama'at Islamiyah—the largest of the two Egyptian terrorist organizations. Hamza had followed the traditional Islamist path: a degree in computer science from Cairo

University, a stint in prison in the wake of Sadat's assassination, and then graduation from the jihad in Afghanistan. He had connections with the mujahideen exiled in Khartoum, and it seemed that members of both Gama'at and the jihad group had cooperated on the Ethiopian operation. At least that was the version presented by Cairo, which also argued that the government of Sudan was directly implicated. Not only did the Sudanese government (sympathetic to the Muslim Brotherhood, a party banned in Egypt) give shelter to radical Egyptian Islamists, but also Sudanese agents in Ethiopia were accused of providing logistical support to the assailants.

The accusation stuck, and Egypt spurred international outrage against Khartoum. A resolution of the United Nations Security Council, adopted in January 1996, imposed sanctions on Sudan. That same month, the CIA Counterterrorism Center set up a special cell to monitor Bin Laden, who was at the time seen as a financier for Islamist terrorists. The fallout of the attack in Addis Ababa was a diplomatic disaster for Khartoum, struggling in the difficult civil war in the south, a conflict often depicted in the international arena as a war between Islam and Christianity. The sanctions immediately tested the relationship between the Sudanese president and the Islamists, and the true nature of the regime was about to be revealed.

The outcome could have been predicted from a previous incident in August 1994, when French agents were allowed to fly into Khartoum to take delivery of "Carlos," wanted in relation to a 1975 shootout in Paris. With the Carlos affair, the Sudanese government hoped to gain credit with the international community for cooperating against terrorism. Raison d'état had ruled then, and it would rule again. A round of parliamentary elections in March 1996 allowed President Bashir to rid the government of the most ideological and internationalist elements of Al-Turabi's party. As for Bin Laden, he had become a tradable commodity for the Sudanese president.

Some accounts report that the Saudi was offered to the highest bidder, but in the end it was the Gulf States—most likely the United Arab Emirates—that acted first. When Bin Laden left Khartoum for Jalalabad, in May 1996, arrangements were made for his chartered plane to refuel in the Persian Gulf—some accounts place the stopover in Qatar, others in the Emirates. The United Arab Emirates, one of only three states to recognize the regime of the Taliban, could have eased his way to safety in Afghanistan. The Egyptians were evicted without further ado. The pretext was a story right out of a spy novel: the sons of mujahideen had been drugged by Egyptian agents, compromised in a sex video, and blackmailed to report on the activities of their fathers. Sudanese agents discovered the plot, and turned the two young men over to the jihad group, which tried and executed them. The whole affair had taken place on Sudanese soil, and the hosts chose to take offense at the execution.

Sudan was not a beacon for the Islamic caliphate: it had been exposed as the true military dictatorship it was, ready to discard militants and ideologues if they became a liability. Sadiq al-Mahdi would remain in and out of house arrest until he escaped to Eritrea in 1999. Al-Turabi would alternate between stints in prison and house arrest. Al Qaeda's moment in the land of the Nubians had passed, leaving behind a faint legacy.

The Egyptian mujahideen were at the end of their rope. Mubarak was well on the way to terminally breaking Gama'at, and that would be the end of the Islamic Revolution in Egypt, the land of Sayyid Qutb. The Russians had released Al-Zawahiri from prison after a few months because he was a man of no importance. His next move would be to Afghanistan, where he would have to lend his services to Bin Laden and the Taliban, and swallow the pill of a suicidal confrontation with the United States. Other mujahideen leaders, more clairvoyant, had rejected the outrageous strategic decision made by the Saudi. But Al-Zawahiri was on the way of binding the fate of the Egyptian jihad group with Bin Laden's grand vision, rationalizing the shift in focus from the "near enemy" to the "far enemy": the United States. It is this transition to a global strategy that would see the Arabic "mujahideen" Latinized as "jihadists."

In 1996, Hassan al-Turabi was a far more famous name than Osama bin Laden in the world of the Islamists. But by losing his grip on power, the Sudanese scholar opened a door for the Saudi handler to grasp the mantle of global leadership. Unlike Al-Turabi, Bin Laden lacked the credentials of a jurist, but he had a sense for theatrics. Getting back on the horse, he gave himself the privilege to issue a fatwa in August 1996. The long, programmatic document was titled "Declaration of War against the Americans Occupying the Land of the Two Holy Places." It would be followed in 1998 by another declaration that established a "World Islamic Front for Jihad against Jews and Crusaders"—the jihadist "federation" sketched out in the early years in Sudan. The latter document would be signed by the leaders of Egyptian, Pakistani, and Bengali groups—all of whom were associates from the time of the Afghan jihad. The ambitions for the Front were to go beyond that circle, to bring in Muslim fighters from all parts of the *Ummah* ("the Community of Believers").

Words without deeds carry little meaning, especially from a man who was not a respected cleric. To be taken seriously Bin Laden had to make good on his threats. There were odd incidents in Saudi Arabia during that period. In November 1995, a car bomb exploded in Riyadh outside a U.S. training facility, killing five Americans. In June 1996, a far more powerful truck bomb was detonated in a residential complex in Al-Khobar, a Saudi town by the Arabian Gulf. The tower targeted by the assailants housed American airmen, nineteen of whom were killed in the blast. The Saudis equivocated, blaming a local Hezbollah manipulated by Iran—a Shia trail that would eventually be accepted by the Clinton administration. Culprits were rapidly executed. Iranian and Shia motivations for killing Americans in Saudi Arabia in the mid-1990s would forever remain unexplained.

Bombings against Israeli and Jewish targets in Argentina in 1992 and 1994 had also been attributed to Lebanese Shias connected to Iran, without any conclusive evidence—and the charges have been consistently denied by Tehran. In hindsight, it is apparent that something was amiss in the early 1990s, that there was a pattern of unclaimed transnational attacks against American and Jewish targets: Buenos Aires, 1992; Aden, 1992; New York, 1993; Buenos Aires, 1994; Riyadh, 1995; and Al-Khobar, 1996. But with the exception of the New York attack, poor investigations and government obfuscation made it impossible to establish responsibility with certainty. Also, the transnational pattern was lost in the noise of local terrorist attacks in relation to conflicts active during those years: Israel, Lebanon, Algeria, Egypt, Bosnia, Chechnya, and Kashmir. It was easier to point at the usual suspect: Tehran, which had done well by state-sponsored transnational terrorism in the 1980s.

Osama bin Laden finally stepped into the limelight as his own man in August 1998, with spectacular, simultaneous truck-bomb attacks against the American Embassies in Nairobi and Dar es Salaam. According to some sources, in the month immediately preceding the attacks, four members of the Egyptian jihad group had been arrested in Albania and turned over—"rendered"—to Egypt by the CIA. This offered a pretext for the embassy bombings, and pointed once more to the Egyptians as perpetrators. But the planning of this relatively complex operation must have predated the arrest of the four men. There were the trucks to be purposely rebuilt, the explosives to be brought in, and the location to be cased. In addition, the date—August 7—marked the beginning of Operation Desert Shield: the deployment of American forces in Saudi Arabia that had so aggrieved Osama bin Laden.

The origins of the militants implicated in the 1998 embassy attacks evokes the cosmopolitan nature of global jihadists: Abdullah Ahmed Abdullah, an Egyptian; Mohammed Saddiq Odeh, a Palestinian; Khalfan Khamis Mohamed, a Tanzanian; Ahmed Salim Swedan, a Kenyan; Wadih El-Hage, a Lebanese raised in Kuwait and a convert to Islam; Mohamed Rashid al-Owhali, a Saudi; Saif al-Adel, an Egyptian; Fazul Abdullah Mohammed, a Comorian; Saleh Ali Saleh Nabhan, a Kenyan; Tariq Abdullah, a Sudanese; Ahmed Khalfan Ghailani, a Tanzanian; and Harun Fadhl, a Comorian. This was a large operation involving many people, from the muscles driving the trucks to a narrow circle of cadres who had been close to Bin Laden. Before settling in Nairobi, El-Hage had worked as a secretary to the Saudi in Sudan, in 1992–94. Al-Adel was a central figure of Al Qaeda: a former officer in the Egyptian Special Forces, a veteran of the Afghan War, and a member of the Shura Council. He would become a central character in the chapters written after the 2001 invasion of Afghanistan.

In 1998, two different trails led from the embassy bombings to Somalia: the "before" and the "after" trails. In the "before" group were Saif al-Adel, Abdullah Ahmed Abdullah, and Mohammed Saddiq Odeh, three men indicted in the 1998 attacks who had also sojourned in Somalia in the early 1990s, where they were allegedly involved in training local radicals. A fourth man, the Comorian Harun Fadhl, was in Mogadishu around the same time, exploring the feasibility of a truck-bomb attack against UN targets. The "before" trail was really about Al Qaeda training operations in Somalia. Much has been made of a camp in Ras Kamboni, a town down the Somali coast, on a small peninsula that pushes out from swamps into the sea, only a few kilometers away from the Kenyan border. According to one version, it was visited by the retainers of Hawiye warlord Mohammed Farah Aidid, the men who would fight U.S. Rangers in Mogadishu in 1993. A more common account is that the camp was used to train the Somali Islamist group Al-Ittihad al-Islami, then at war with Ethiopia.

The Ras Kamboni camp may have been real, and it may even have been frequented by Al-Ittihad. But the claim that the camp was run by Al Qaeda and that Al-Ittihad was directed by Al Qaeda seems unsubstantiated. Saif al-Adel, who had previously been involved in training operations, instructed in late 1992 Mohammed Saddiq Odeh, a junior figure, to look for opportunities to set up training facilities in Somalia. Odeh does not seem to have done much more than spend a few months with a tribe, sharing techniques about small-arms usage and battlefield medicine. The foreign jihadists of Al Qaeda did not start a war between Somalia and Ethiopia: it is commonly accepted that Eritrea had been behind Al-Ittihad all along. And the foreign jihadists of Al Qaeda did not take down American helicopters during the Battle of Mogadishu: the men of the warlord Aidid did.

In the early 1990s, Al Qaeda was not more than mujahideen in exile with some experience and connections. The most they could bring to a conflict area were good wishes, a few fighters, and their contacts with the Islamic charities and relief organizations that had supported them during the Afghan jihad. In those years, Bin Laden was still seen as a money man, not as a warrior in his own right. It is not very plausible that seasoned Somali warriors would train in their own country in a foreign outfit, however experienced those foreigners may have been, let alone take orders from those foreigners. The venture in Somalia of the "before" group was a reconnaissance mission, and it did not amount to much. As for the "after" group, three suspects in the embassy attacks found shelter in Somalia after 1998: Fazul Abdullah Mohammed, Tariq Abdullah, and Saleh Ali Saleh Nabhan. Their presence there would attract close American scrutiny and would crucially shape U.S. policy toward Somalia in the decade that followed. Their path will be traced in a subsequent chapter.

Abu Ubaidah al-Banshiri, an Egyptian born in 1950, was at the time Al Qaeda's second in command and had led the African cell for Bin Laden until his accidental death, in 1996, at which point a younger man, Abdullah Ahmed Abdullah, had assumed a leadership role. But it was just that: a cell, whose existence had been driven toward and had come to a climax with the 1998 embassy attacks. Convenience is the best explanation for the selection of Kenya and Tanzania as targets for the bombings. Following the unraveling of the Afghan War, that cohort of militants had settled along an elliptical axis running from Saudi Arabia to Sudan, via Yemen, Kenya, and Somalia. Nairobi and Dar es Salaam were targets of opportunity. Evicted from Sudan and restricted in

Saudi Arabia, jihadists would come out where they could, first in Africa in 1998, and then, a couple of years later, on the other shore of the Bab el-Mandeb, in the port of Aden. Those countries were neither hotbeds of Islamist radicalism nor failed states passed under the control of transnational terrorists. Too weak to be police states and too densely populated for a few interlopers to stand out, they were simply places where operatives could move around.

The strategic purpose of the 1998 operation, besides making Osama bin Laden a household name, was to provoke retaliation. Not everyone in the upper echelons of the mujahideen movement was sanguine about the wisdom of confronting the United States. There were vocal opponents to the 1998 attacks, as there would be vocal opponents to the 2001 attacks, from men who predicted the devastation that would be unleashed upon their assets worldwide. But their fears in 1998 were excessive. Retaliation did come from the Clinton administration in a form that would be later described—by President George W. Bush—as sending multimillion-dollar missiles to knock over empty 10-dollar tents. A pharmaceutical factory in Sudan was bombed; it was later established it made nothing but medications. Osama bin Laden and the mujahideen had come and gone. For Al Qaeda, the 1998 bombing was a farewell to Africa. In the days that preceded the operation, the main cadres had left the region and scurried for cover in Pakistan. This is where American forces would find them in due time. But before that, the provocation had to be stepped up.

CHAPTER FIVE

War at Sea

T HERE WAS NOTHING ORIGINAL in the principle. Egypt had done it in the late 1960s, with the closure of the Suez Canal. Iran had done it in the late 1980s, laying mines and attacking shipping in the Arabian Gulf. But it had never been done by a non-state actor before, and so the plan carried the fanciful ambition characteristic of Al Qaeda. Osama bin Laden had always been concerned with the price of oil, which he felt was artificially low as a result of collusion between the Saudi royals and the United States. A foreign power was orchestrating the plunder of the wealth of Muslims. Al Qaeda was not going to shut down the Bab el-Mandeb. But slowing down shipping between the Mediterranean and the Arabian Sea had a shot at bringing the price of a barrel of oil closer to its fair market value. It would be an act of justice.

The first act of the naval campaign was to coincide with the so-called millennium plot—a cluster of operations planned for execution around the final week of 1999. The target was the *USS The Sullivans*, an American destroyer calling in the port of Aden. It was a dinghy-based variation on the suicide truck bomb used in the 1998 American Embassy attacks. The operation took place on January 3, 2000—it went unnoticed, the dinghy sinking under the weight of the explosives it carried before getting close enough to the ship. The other operations of the millennium, in Los Angeles and Amman, also failed. As the century closed, Al Qaeda had two successes—the 1993 attack against the World Trade Center and the 1998 African Embassy bombings—among a long series of operational failures.

It is difficult to establish the extent to which all three "millennium" operations were coordinated, but the coincidental timing, the operational design, and the personal history of some of the plotters, linking them to the mujahideen milieu, suggest a shared vision. On Christmas Eve 2000 there would be an attempted bombing of a cathedral in France and several bombings of churches in Indonesia, followed within days by a wave of bombings in Manila, Philippines. It could have been coincidence, but the pattern would repeat itself in 2001. That year's Al Qaeda season opened early, with the September attacks in New York and Washington. There were follow-up operations planned in Paris, Rome, and Singapore—all foiled. And there would be yet another wave in 2002 against tourist resorts in Djerba (April), Bali (October), and Mombasa (November). That year would mark the end of the operational activity of Al Qaeda proper—Khalid Sheikh Mohammed, the master of operations, was captured in March 2003 in Rawalpindi.

The naval component of the activity of those years was based in Aden, Yemen. Learning from the January 2000 fiasco against the *USS The Sullivans*, the same group was able to bring a small craft laden with C4 explosives against another destroyer refueling in Aden, the *USS Cole*. The date was October 12, 2000. The craft was steered by two suicide bombers, both Yemenis, who waved as they approached. The blast caused a gaping hole in the hull of the ship, killing 17 sailors lined up for lunch in the galley behind. A political message had been sent about the presence of the American fleet in the Arabian Sea. A reminder message was to come two years later, in October 2002, with a similar operation against a French tanker, the *Limburg*. This time the attack was carried out far at sea and left no witnesses. There would be one victim, and the ship's hull would be similarly torn, releasing crude oil in the Gulf of Aden.

The lesson of those operations is that Al Qaeda operatives showed remarkable tenacity, ingenuity, and ambition given their limited means. Following the attack against the *USS Cole*, Yemeni authorities had investigated in the local mujahideen milieu, casting a wide net and rounding up suspects for questioning. One man on the list was Khalid al-Mihdhar, a Saudi born in 1975 who had fought in Bosnia in the 1990s. Al-Mihdhar had been in Aden visiting his wife in the months preceding the 2000 bombing of the *USS Cole*. Before that, he had sojourned in California. It was during his time in San Diego, while learning to fly jets, that Al-Mihdhar frequented a mosque where he met local Imam Anwar al-Awlaki, who himself would later move to Yemen and earn a reputation as an advocate for jihad. A well-known jihadist, Al-Mihdhar was questioned about the *USS*

Cole, but this operation was not his and he soon left Yemen to meet his fate. Al-Mihdhar would die a year later as one of the 9/11 hijackers.

Yemen would charge six men in the naval attack. They were placed at the scene but seemed low on the chain of command; some were mere accessories. Yemen refused to extradite them to the United States and issued light sentences for four of the men. Washington was not satisfied and pursued the investigation. Years later, a U.S. federal judge would condemn the Sudanese government for providing the attackers with material support—such as passports and diplomatic pouches—an unlikely accusation designed to allow the release of Sudanese assets frozen in the United States to the families of the victims. Eventually, a trail emerged that led to Osama bin Laden by way of a Saudi of Yemeni origin named Abd al-Rahim al-Nashiri. Al-Nashiri, the probable leader of the cell, was born in 1965 in the Hijaz, the more cosmopolitan region of the west coast of Saudi Arabia. He is said to have fought in Afghanistan in the glorious days of the jihad against the Soviet Union, and returned again in the mid-1990s to fight in Tajikistan. At some point he joined forces with Bin Laden. He moved to Yemen around 1998 to establish a cell there. A close relative of his is thought to have been among the suicide bombers of the 1998 embassy attacks in Africa.

1998 was also the year a group of Yemeni salafis led by a 32-year-old Abu al-Hassan, who is believed to have been a graduate of the Afghan jihad, made itself known to the world as the Islamic Army of Abyan-Aden—Abyan being the maritime province immediately east of Aden. The new-comer Islamic Army, which had issued threats against for-eigners, abducted 16 Western tourists on December 28. The hostage takers protested the recent aerial bombing of Iraq by British and American forces as part of Operation Desert Fox, and demanded the release of a leader of their group who was recently captured. The incident was a fiasco for the Yemeni government, whose forces killed four hostages in a rescue operation. Al-Hassan was captured and executed the following October by order of President Saleh. His Islamic Army perished with him.

There is scant evidence that Al-Hasan was connected to the group responsible for the naval attacks in Aden, let alone to the Al Qaeda leadership. The Islamic Army was loud, and its single operation a poorly planned failure. By contrast, the Nashiri cell was discreet and focused on opera-tional success. Al-Nashiri had left Yemen a few days before the attack on the *USS Cole* and had called in an underling from the United Arab Emirates, ordering the operation be executed. The underling was Jamal al-Badawi, a Yemeni and one of six men convicted in the attack. Al-Badawi and Al-Nashiri were condemned to death by the Yemeni govern-ment in 2004. But Al-Nashiri was tried *in absentia* and the fate of Al-Badawi was not sealed yet. The man would reap-pear later.

Al-Nashiri, the operational planner, was not captured until November 2002, one month after the attack on the *Limburg* tanker. Arrested in the United Arab Emirates, he would be transferred to the Guantanamo detention center but never charged because of the conditions under which he was interrogated. Another man that the United States had identified as a suspect in the attack, Ali Qaed Senyan al-Harthi, a Yemeni national and former mujahideen, was killed the same month Al-Nashiri was arrested. He was riding in a car in the Ma'rib province of Yemen when he made a claim on history for being the first victim of a drone attack conducted by the CIA. Scores were being settled for the *USS Cole.*

The October 2002 attack against the *Limburg* had limited economic consequences, at least outside Yemen. The increase in the price of oil was short-lived, but the increase in insurance premiums for ships calling at Aden reduced local traffic, which hurt the local economy. The members of the Nashiri cell were Yemenis and Saudis, mujahideen veterans of the Afghan War. It was a hard generation, inured to the merciless nature of jihad. Born in the 1960s, their youth was spent in the years before the oil wealth, and they had come of age fighting Russians, far from the indulgent consumerism of boom-era Saudi Arabia. They were a different lot from the next generation, the impressionable or impecunious young men they would recruit from around the world for the jihad, often as cannon fodder in suicide operations. That earlier generation was ready to die, but it didn't fight with death in mind. That generation had rancor, and it had purpose.

At the end of 2002, with Al-Badawi and Al-Nashiri incarcerated and Al-Harthi dead, the naval cell was for all intents and purposes shut down. Al Qaeda would return to Yemen, but the curtain had closed on that second act—the first act being the hotel attacks in 1992 and the cell around Tariq al-Fadhli. In March 2003, U.S. forces entered Iraq, and the focus of jihad moved there and to the Afghan-Pakistan border. But the idea of sabotaging oil commerce and disrupting sea-lanes lingered. In 2004, the militant group led from inside Iraq by Jordanian Abu Musab al-Zarqawi bombed two offshore oil terminals near Basra, claiming responsibility for the attacks with reference to the *USS Cole* and *Limburg* precedents. In August 2005, American vessels docked in Aqaba, Jordan, came under rocket fire from a group that called itself the Abdullah Azzam Brigades, after the legendary Palestinian mujahideen. In July 2010, a Japanese tanker sailing past Hormuz, in the Arabian Gulf, suffered damage to its hull from an explosion reminiscent of the *Limburg modus operandi*.

As a Turkish proverb puts it: the dogs bark, and the caravan goes by. Naval attacks from jihadists barely made an impression on the intense shipping traffic in the region. That achievement would go to old-fashioned pirates. The Red Sea and the Gulf of Aden have always been a hive of maritime activity beyond the reach of states. In the nineteenth century, piracy, slave trading, and gunrunning were taxing British attempts to pacify the region and abolish human trafficking. Largely to control this traffic, the British established protectorates along the coast so that their agents could monitor activity in local ports and impose on the sultans to act when laws were broken at sea. *Pax Britannica* had come. When *Pax Britannica* left in the 1960s, the duty

of regulating maritime activity fell on newly independent states that were ill-equipped to do so militarily and
politically.

Nights on the Red Sea and Arabian Sea belong to the
speedboats of smugglers and their contraband of drugs, cig-
arettes, and small arms. Arms are mostly shipped on a large
scale from Yemen to Somalia, and some are smuggled back
into Yemen to supply local insurgents. There is also human
traffic going the other way: Sudanese, Ethiopians, and
Somalis seeking reprieve from poverty and the violence of
the Horn of Africa cross the strait at night, looking to reach
Yemen. Occasionally, dozens are lost at sea in tragic acci-
dents. Of the tens of thousands who make it across the Bab
el-Mandeb into Yemen, witnesses describe boats hurriedly
beached and refugees jumping overboard and running to
escape capture by the army. Those who get caught would be
trucked north to the Saudi border and sold to contractors.
Overpopulated Yemen, while better than Somalia, makes
for a poor country of asylum. Hopes of a better life lie in
the oil-rich countries of the Gulf, but the traffic is brutal.
Some young girls pay a heavy price for that dream.

The Republic of Somalia has more than 3,000 kilometers
(2,000 miles) of coast peppered with seaports and small
fishing towns. The Somali navy had never been much to
begin with, but with the collapse of the state in 1991, Somalis were no longer in a position to enforce sovereign maritime claims and protect their national resources, the rich
waters of the Arabian Sea. Spanish, French, Thai, South

Korean, and Japanese high-seas trawlers, the usual suspects of global industrial fishing, started prowling Somali waters for valuable catches of tuna, shark, and lobster. With their livelihood threatened, armed local fishermen responded by boarding the foreign ships. The captains paid the Somalis for "protection" to complete their campaigns. By the turn of the century, those raids evolved quite naturally into piracy.

The phenomenon of piracy was to remain scattered, with distinct groups distributed along the coast. Some piratical outfits retained their vigilante origins: a self-appointed National Volunteer Coast Guard, operating from the southern port of Kismayo, has claimed to focus only on illegal fishing and on ships dumping toxic waste. But by and large, the defense of Somali waters had become an excuse for widespread mugging and racketeering. Pirates, claiming to be Somali marines, indiscriminately boarded fishing, recreational, and commercial vessels, looking to plunder. Eventually, a few operations became more ambitious and, from around 2005, turned to ransoming larger and larger vessels seized far beyond Somali coastal waters.

Ransoming foreign ships required holding the captured vessels for an extended period of time, sometimes several months, in a sanctuary within Somali territorial waters. For that, pirates needed protection on land, for they were never sovereign. For all the weakness of local governments, the prosperity of the piratical trade depended on the acquiescence of local power brokers. Financial accommodations were made to get local populations, religious leaders, and officials onboard. Clan-based relationships helped facilitate those arrangements. The pirates could bribe their way only so far. They never made it to the large seaports, but operated from smaller beach ports along the coast. From north to south, the main centers were in Eyl, in Puntland; in Xarardheere-Hobyo, north of Mogadishu; and in Marka, south of Mogadishu. Somaliland, which has made a point of displaying attributes of sovereignty in its quest for international recognition, did not allow pirates to operate from its territory. By contrast, many captured vessels were diverted to Eyl because local authorities could be bribed and Puntland provided a degree of security that was absent in the troubled south.

Revenue from piracy was an economic bonanza, even though only a fraction of the money was spent locally, mostly on khat and weapons. A few armed retainers and new concrete houses in the beach towns of Somalia were the physical manifestation of piratical success. The senior partners in piratical ventures were wise enough to recycle their profits in safer hubs like Mombasa, Dubai, and Mumbai. Ransom money purchased villas in faraway lands. The main operators were well known: Mohamed Abdi Hassan "Afweyne" ("Big Mouth") was a favorite of the international media. He operated from his base in Xarardheere-Hobyo, second only to Eyl as a piratical center. Besides Afweyne, Farah Hirsi Kulan "Boyah" and Garaad Mohamud Mohamed were on a short list of Somali entrepreneurs in high-seas piracy. This testifies to the limited scale and visibility of their operations. Pirates did not have to hide, and there was not much to hide: they were all low-tech, low-cost operations.

In the south, piracy developed within the broader context of statelessness and civil war, and its fortunes ebbed and flowed following local developments. After the Islamic Courts Union took control of Mogadishu in the summer of 2006, armed men were sent to take Xarardheere. The pirates disbanded and the number of attacks at sea dropped in the following months. With the Ethiopian invasion at the end of that year and the subsequent civil war that absorbed both the Ethiopian camp and the Islamists, the pirates—members of a local subclan—returned to Xarardheere with a vengeance. This is when their activity peaked, and they started making international headlines.

What made Somali pirates an overnight global sensation were two attacks at the end of 2008. In September, they seized a Ukrainian freighter carrying Cold War-era military equipment, from grenade launchers to Russian T-72 tanks. The ship was bound for Kenya, but the destination of the weapons was the secessionist government of South Sudan. Soviet tanks would have been of no use to either pirates or terrorists and presented no threats to international security, but the exposure of the clandestine arms deal was an international embarrassment, and a reminder of the volatility of that part of Africa. Then, in November of that year, the capture of the *Sirius Star*, a high-capacity Saudi tanker carrying 2 million barrels of crude, was a reminder of the importance of those sea-lanes for the uninterrupted supply of oil to Europe. Both ships, their cargoes, and their crews were released after a few months, for a ransom of about $3 million each.

Publicity of that kind made the work of Somali pirates more difficult. What really doomed them were abductions for ransom that involved nationals of Western powers. In April 2009, the container vessel *Maersk Alabama* was tentatively boarded by pirates, before being recaptured by the crew, who also rammed and sank the assailants' skiff. The pirates escaped on a lifeboat, taking as hostage the captain, a U.S. citizen. A few days later, Navy Seals shot three of the four captors during a rescue operation. Instances where Western militaries would go after pirates with lethal force had been rare, but there was a legal footing to intervene when nationals were taken hostage. There also was political value in showing strength in such cases. In April 2008, Somali pirates had captured the crew of a French luxury yacht, *Le Ponant*. Ransom was paid and the crew released, but French commandos followed the pirates, captured them on land, and brought them to France for trial.

The piracy threat to shipping was manageable. There was economic loss, whether in the form of higher premiums or ransom, but the cost was marginal compared to the total value of goods transiting the region. About 20,000 ships cross the Bab el-Mandeb every year. In a bad year, 200 are attacked, with only a fraction actually seized. But pirates were becoming more daring, operating farther out at sea. By 2009, they were using mother ships from which they would launch their skiffs against targets as far off as the coast of Kenya and the Seychelles. Ships had also been attacked in Yemeni and Omani waters, although the pirates there may have been locals. Assessment of the pirates' fleet should be kept in line with reality: The so-called "mother ships" are mostly small diesel tankers that allow the pirates to stay out and refuel at sea; the skiffs are black-painted aluminum or wooden shells with powerful outboard engines of the kind used by smugglers throughout the Indian Ocean. Their operations are cheap, but effective.

Reaction came from the sea. The American-led Combined Task Force 150 had been operating in the Arabian Sea in relation to the War on Terror and Operation Enduring Freedom. While piracy was not their main focus, American vessels had occasionally engaged pirates after 2005. A March 2006 skirmish had resulted in the death and capture of Somalis, but those events were rare. In mid-2008, the European Union, mandated by new UN resolutions and at the request of the Transitional Government of Somalia, set up Operation Atalanta. European naval forces would sail off the coast of Somalia to protect the delivery of aid from the World Food Program and to assist ships threatened by pirates. NATO countries pledged to contribute to the effort. At the end of that year, China sent three ships to the area. Then, in early 2009, the U.S. assigned to a new Task Force 151 the mission to confront pirates off Somalia, with support from South Korea and other allies. NATO Operation "Ocean Shield" commenced in August. Suddenly, Somalia had become a highly visible testing ground for navies, and fighting piracy was a must-do for states with ambitions of becoming a global power.

Those efforts worked to a point. In the spring of 2009, French commandos boarded a small sailboat, the *Tanit*, to rescue a family held captive by pirates. A Dutch ship freed Belgian hostages, and a Portuguese ship rescued Norwegians under attack by pirates. The French preemptively captured pirates at sea on several occasions. The larger commercial vessels had found methods to thwart the assailants: when they could not outrun or outmaneuver them, they used water cannons, sonic weapons, and even armed guards. A private security guard would cause a stir in March 2010 by shooting and killing a Somali trying to board the ship. Yet the numerous interventions by Western navies failed to prevent a still-significant number of vessels from being captured and ransomed. The rate of failed boardings had increased, but so had the rate of attempted boardings.

The Somalis factored the extra risk into their analysis and found it profitable to continue, using larger mother ships captured at sea and spreading over greater expanses of ocean to avoid the foreign patrols. Deterrence at sea had shown its limits, especially with incidents like that of the *Tanit*, where a hostage was accidentally killed during the rescue operation.

A British couple captured in 2009 near the Seychelles would be held captive for over a year, until relatives were able to put together a payment. The biggest payoff at the time—almost $10 million—was obtained in November 2010 in return for a South Korean oil tanker, the *Samho Dream*, held for several months in Hobyo. A January 2011 special report to the United Nations conceded that the naval effort had failed. Various studies estimated the yearly costs from the activity of Somali pirates in excess of $5 billion. Almost 1,200 hostages had been taken in 2010 and held an average 213 days. In January 2011, unnerved South Korean commandos killed eight pirates—and the ship's captain—while storming the *Samho Jewelry*, a chemical carrier seized the week before. In February, pirates killed four American hostages held on a yacht because they were shadowed by an U.S. Navy Destroyer. This was not an accident but a deliberate message to deter future rescue operations. Hostage-taking and execution was now at the core of the *modus operandi* of Somali pirates. In April, they claimed a new record ransom: $13.5 million paid for a Greek tanker captured along the coast of Oman, the *Irene SL*.

The real effort had to come from land, enrolling and building up local authorities to stop the pirates from taking to sea. There were legal problems aplenty: the Western countries whose navies had captured pirates at sea generally had no jurisdiction to prosecute, and pirates could not be tried nor imprisoned in their own country for lack of a functioning judicial system. The vast majority of them had to be released. Financial incentives were made available to the countries in the region willing to aid a collective effort to contain piracy. Kenya was enrolled to try and hold pirates captive. Djibouti, as a base for Western forces, was another prime beneficiary of strategic rent derived from the piratical threat. Somaliland, while still denied recognition as an independent state, obtained financial and military help to build its own embryonic naval forces. The authorities in Puntland were offered incentives to shut down the piratical operations in Eyl, but little progress was made. The January 2011 report to the United Nations recommended stepping up the effort. It proposed that an extraterritorial court be set up in Arusha, Tanzania, and provided for special courts and prisons in Somaliland and Puntland. The plan was an acknowledgment that little could be done with regard to southern Somalia, endemically lawless. The epitome of irony was reached in June 2011, when the Western-backed Transitional Government of Somalia seized $3.6 million in ransom money flown into the country by the couriers of a security firm. Pirates operated in the first place because the government was inept, and now the government was racketeering the victims of piracy—imposing a $100,000 fine on top of the cash it confiscated.

The absence of central authority in southern Somalia had not spared pirates from having to contend with local opposition: imams who disapproved of brigandage and parents whose sons were recruited for the dangerous missions at sea. Local religious authorities were often fierce opponents, and they could rally enough armed supporters to intimidate the pirates. But the evolving situation at the turn of the decade made pirates sought-after allies for local communities. With the towns north of Mogadishu threatened by the radical Islamists rampaging through the southernmost areas, pirates appeared as the lesser of two evils. They could be drafted to join in the protection of the town. And the pirates had learned the lessons of 2006, when the Islamists had gone after them. To protect their bases on land, they now invested larger amounts of ransom money to buy weapons and hire retainers. The pirates were building up militias to fight the Islamists if need be, and the militias were becoming dependent on piracy.

CHAPTER SIX

The Rise of the Shabab

THE BATTLE OF MOGADISHU in the summer of 2006 established the Islamic Courts Union as the dominant player in south Somalia. Its success dealt a blow to Ethiopia's ability to manipulate the course of events through the weak Transitional Federal Government it had backed since 2000. If Sharif Shaykh Ahmed, the leader of the Executive Committee of the Courts, appeared as a prudent man, the presence of Hassan Dahir Aweys, the military leader of the Courts, was ominous. Aweys was the same man who had waged an irregular war against Ethiopia for most of the 1990s, as leader of the militant group Al-Ittihad al-Islami. His attitude in the summer of 2006 was defiant when he talked of eliminating the Transitional Federal Government and keeping up the fight until all Somali provinces—and that meant the Ogaden—were united into a Greater Somalia. Ethiopia had invaded Somalia once before in 1996 to take him out of the Gedo region; it could invade again to take him out of Mogadishu.

On the surface, the United States had no dog in that fight. But the Bush administration had never warmed up to the Courts, which it felt could, like the Taliban, provide a haven for Al Qaeda. The presence of former Al-Ittihad cadres in key positions within the Courts' militia was a disturbing signal. If anything linked Al-Ittihad to Al Qaeda, it was the career of Aden Hashi Farah ("Ayro"), a protégé of Aweys who, according to the International Crisis Group, had trained in Afghanistan in the years leading to 2001. He would become a principal of the youth movement of the Islamic Courts—Harakat al-Shabab Mujahideen ("Movement of the Combatant Youth").

For Washington, the interest in Somalia was to capture Al Qaeda operatives and bring closure to the 1998 attacks against the American Embassies. Two CIA personnel had been killed in Nairobi, and in a page taken from the book of Israeli counterterrorism, the accounts for those deaths would be methodically settled by extrajudicial killings. It would take thirteen years—and the execution of Osama bin Laden in Abbottabad, Pakistan, would not even be the end of it.

With regard Somalia, there was the trail of the three indicted men who had found shelter there. One of them was the Sudanese Tariq Abdullah, known as Abu Taha. Abu Taha had re-emerged in November 2002 as a planner of the suicide attack against a Mombasa seaside resort, immediately followed by an attempt to shoot down an Israeli charter plane with surface-to-air missiles. Al Qaeda had returned to Africa, and Abu Taha was the point man. Abu Taha was married to a Somali woman, and following the 2002 attack in Kenya, he had moved to Mogadishu. There, he had teamed up with a Somali named Gouled Hassan

Dourad. Dourad had trained in Afghanistan in the 1990s and then joined Al-Ittihad al-Islami around 1997. In 2003, the two men were together in Mogadishu and suspected of planning an attack against the new American base in Djibouti. Gouled Dourad was captured in Mogadishu in 2004 by a Somali warlord and turned over to the CIA. He would show up in Guantanamo a couple of years later. The U.S. government wanted Abu Taha as well and is said to have required assistance from the Courts Union, but the Sudanese remained at large. The Bush administration had made the strategic decision to get more involved in Africa. In 2002, a military base was leased in Djibouti. In 2003, $100 million was allocated to the East Africa Counterterrorism Initiative. Washington found allies in the region: Kenya and Ethiopia. It was an alliance of convenience rather than ideology. American diplomats saw through the radicalism of Ethiopian nationalism and the self-interest of a government preoccupied by the everlasting proxy war with Eritrea—a war fought in the rebellious Ethiopian provinces, in Somalia, and in Sudan. A 2009 U.S. diplomatic cable from Addis Ababa reports lucidly on the efforts of hardliners in (Christian) Ethiopia to push Washington to reconcile with the (Islamic) regime of Sudanese President Bashir—the first acting head of state to be under an arrest warrant from the International Criminal Court for crimes of genocide. The reason was that Asmara was helping the secessionist rebels of southern Sudan, in the same way that it was supporting the Oromo and Ogadeni rebels in Ethiopia. For Addis Ababa, the fight against terrorism meant crushing all the secessionist movements of Eastern Africa, and their Eritrean lifeline.

Ethiopia's agenda for Somalia in the mid-2000s was the faltering Transitional Government. At the risk of undermining the modicum of social order the Islamic Courts had managed to impose in Mogadishu, Washington decided to go along. The first step was to give firepower to the Transitional Government, which was accomplished through the creation of an ungainly named Alliance for the Restoration of Peace and Counterterrorism, which is hardly more palatable in the Somali *Isbaheysiga La dagaalanka Argagixisadda.* The Alliance, widely reported as being financed by the CIA, was a hodgepodge of clan-based militias, Somali businessmen, and warlords. A leader of the Alliance was Mohamed Omar Habeb, a warlord appointed governor of Mogadishu in the mid-1990s by Aidid—the same Aidid who had fought the Americans in 1993.

The die was cast: it would be the Alliance backed by America and Ethiopia against the Eritrean-backed Islamic Courts Union. What went down in history as the Second Battle of Mogadishu broke out between the two sides in early 2006. Violence dragged on for a few months, in a series of skirmishes that left hundreds dead and exposed the limits of the Alliance, which was wiped out by the summer. The Islamic Courts Union had tested its power and, for the first time, ran the whole of Mogadishu from which it quickly spread to establish its authority over most of the south. But the success of the Islamic Courts Union, described in a previous chapter, was short-lived. By the summer's end, Washington had agreed to let Ethiopia stir things up. Chaos had its own virtue in comparison to a fundamentalist order with potential jihadist guests.

The crucible for the next act would be the town of Baidoa, west of Mogadishu, over half-way to the Ethiopian border. Baidoa was then the seat of the Transitional Somali Government—a government only in name, holed up in a town under Ethiopian protection. In October, "government" forces backed by Ethiopian elements pushed east of the city to briefly occupy the town of Buur Hakaba, on the road to Mogadishu. Provoked, the Courts Union responded aggressively and fell into the trap, sending its militias, including the Shabab units, to surround Baidoa. The Battle of Baidoa started in mid-December 2006, when Ethiopian troops crossed the border to relieve the besieged Somali government. Success was quick: the Courts Union and its militias, facing Ethiopian firepower, dispersed in a matter of days. Mogadishu was abandoned, and the Somali Islamists retreated toward Kenya. There were last stands all along the withdrawal route to the south: in Jilib, in Kismayo, and finally in Ras Kamboni. Irregular militias were no match for regular units in a war for position, and Somali fighters were forced to cross into Kenya.

The United States had dispatched a few Special Forces to operate inside Somalia, and intelligence agents to filter the flow of refugees at the Kenyan border, hoping to pluck Al Qaeda operatives along with some useful information. The Sudanese Abu Taha, one of the men wanted for the 1998 embassy bombings, had showed up at the battle of Baidoa,

leading a group of fighters for the Islamic Courts Union
near the town of Idale. He was most likely killed in a U.S.
air strike in January 2007 near Ras Kamboni. The turn of
Kenyan Saleh Ali Saleh Nabhan would come in September
2009, when he was the target of a U.S. Special Forces air-
borne operation in Baraawe, a coastal town in southern
Somalia. His body was airlifted to an American ship for
identification. The third graduate of the 1998 embassy
bombings hiding in Somalia, the Comorian Fazul Abdullah
Mohammed ("Harun Fazul"), was believed to have perished at the 2007 battle of Ras Kamboni. But he would meet
his fate accidentally in June 2011, showing up at a wrong
checkpoint in Mogadishu. Surprised to find there troops of
the Transitional Government, he opened fire and was killed
in the shootout. Fazul had been hiding for ten years among
the mixed-race people of coastal Somalia. On his body were
found around forty thousand dollars and a South African
passport. There were rumors that he had helped the Shabab
with a terrorist attack in Uganda, in 2008, and that he was
a contact point between them and al Qaeda in the Arabian
Peninsula, in Yemen. Much about his life was speculative,
but his death, coming a month after that of Bin Laden,
marked the end of an era.

   In early 2007, the Somali Islamists were on the run, but
Ethiopian forces never came close to pacifying Somalia. On
the contrary, abuses of the population and violations of
human rights triggered a humanitarian crisis, and Mogadishu
was drained of the majority of its population. Human Rights
Watch reported 1 million displaced persons, a symbolic

number showing the magnitude of the human tragedy. Political risks soon escaped the borders of the failed state, as the flow of Somali refugees grew from the tens to the hundreds of thousands. Many fled to Kenya, where Somalis were regrouped in cramped refugee camps and abused by the Kenyan police. Others joined the quarter-million Somalis who had found their way illegally into Yemen over the years, where the influx exacerbated an already marginal social situation.

Meanwhile, it did not take long for Somali militias to regroup and pass onto the offensive. War raged throughout 2007 and 2008 between the occupying forces trying to impose the Transitional Federal Government, and groups of Islamists opposing them, reinforced by foreign volunteers responding to the call to join the struggle against Christian Ethiopia and its American backers. The Somali resistance was at first factious and localized, but a couple of identifiable clusters emerged from the struggle. One was led by Aweys, who had along with his sidekick Siad pulled a disappearance act when Mogadishu fell, only to reappear a few months later in Eritrea. There, he led a council of Somali leaders assembled in an Alliance for the Re-liberation of Somalia. The other cluster was Harakat al-Shabab Mujahideen, known to the world as Al-Shabab, the erstwhile youth movement of the Islamic Courts.

Both Aweys' Alliance and the Shabab came from the Courts; they shared an Islamist outlook and were committed to fighting Ethiopia and keeping foreign influence out of Somali affairs. Aweys' Alliance retained the backing of

Eritrea, in keeping with Asmara's policy of harassing Ethiopia at every turn. The origins of material support for the Shabab are more mysterious. The Shabab have presented themselves as sons of the land united by faith, rallying against foreign oppression. They seized their weapons from the dispirited troops of the Transitional Government and raised funds from a supportive populace—or so the story goes. But their effectiveness on the ground against Ethiopian troops belied the image of a spontaneous, popular uprising. There were rumors of sponsorship from sympathetic businessmen in Kenya and in the Arabian Peninsula. As is often the case, it is difficult to discern the genuine money trail from conspiracy theories, but Eritrea may also have hedged its bets by backing both the Shabab and the Alliance. Whatever the case, the Shabab rapidly grew into a powerful force just as they broke away from the trusteeship of Aweys and the Islamic Courts.

If Somali militias were no match for Ethiopian troops in open combat, they knew their way around irregular warfare. With its units constantly harassed, exposed to suicide bombings, and faced with a humanitarian crisis, Ethiopia lost its nerves against the Islamists and began searching for an exit strategy. Negotiations were held in Djibouti throughout 2008, and arrangements were made to bring the more moderate Islamists within the Alliance for the Reliberation of Somalia (the former Islamic Courts Union) into the Transitional Federal Government. Sharif Sheikh Ahmed, who had been the political leader of the Courts

Union and then the figurehead of the anti-Ethiopian alliance, assumed the function of president of Somalia in January 2009. This was the promise of a new era. His regime
was internationally recognized, and foreign aid was made
available. Peacekeepers from Uganda and Burundi,
equipped by the United States and under the aegis of the
African Union, guaranteed the security of the new coalition
government as Ethiopian troops withdrew across the
border.

Sharif Ahmed's vision for Somalia is of a Muslim country
ruled by Shariah, but in the grand scheme of things, he is a
moderate man, willing to work with the West to restore
order in south Somalia. His conciliatory position was
rejected by hard-liners in the Alliance for the Re-liberation
of Somalia, who rallied behind the old warrior Aweys under
the umbrella of a *Hizbul Islam*, or "Islamic Party." Their
defection was not the main challenge to the new government. The Hizbul Islam lacked teeth and cohesion, and its
attempt to fly the religious colors was too little too late: that
niche was already occupied by the Shabab. For it is the Shabab that had done the job of grinding down Ethiopian
troops throughout 2007–2008, and it is the Shabab that
filled the void after their departure. And the Shabab would
have none of the reconciliation process.

The original *amir* ("military leader") of the Shabab came
from Al-Ittihad by way of Afghanistan, where he allegedly
trained in the 1990s. Aden Hashi Farah ("Ayro"), a protégé
of Aweys, was a belligerent character with a flair for the

dramatic. In Afghanistan, he absorbed the fundamentalist practice of the Taliban and Al Qaeda's strategic obsession with foreigners. He brought that attitude back to Somalia around 2003. At first, Ayro led an underground cell in Mogadishu, where he built a reputation killing aid workers and foreign officials. Aweys restrained him with an appointment as principal of the Shabab. The chain of command was clear: Aweys was the head of the Shura Council of the Islamic Courts Union, and the Shabab were an operation of the Courts.

In the summer of 2006, as the Islamic Courts Union savored its success and order returned to southern Somalia, it was reported that Ayro led 700 young Somali fighters to Lebanon to reinforce Hezbollah against Israel—a wild allegation dismissed by the Lebanese as "silly." It seems that Ayro's braggadocio had been taken at face value by monitors reporting to the United Nations. But the incident says something of Ayro's character, and of the value of publicity for global jihadists. The Ethiopian invasion at the end of 2006 gave him free rein, and he ran loose with the Shabab for 18 months until his flamboyance got him killed by a U.S. drone in May 2008.

The man who took over from him, Ahmed Abdi Godane ("Abu Zubeyr"), had a similar pedigree and virulence. Born in 1977 in Somaliland, Godane had gone to study in Pakistan under a Saudi fellowship program, and allegedly transferred from there to Afghanistan under the Taliban. He was back in Hargeisa, the capital of Somaliland, in 2001, preaching at a local mosque and gathering fellow militants. In the following two years, he got involved in the assassination of foreign aid workers. The eruption of violence in Somaliland was concerning to the aspiring state, which had been spared the disruptions of the south. The identity of the victims was also shocking. An Italian nurse, with 30 years of local experience, was killed in 2003 in Boroma, Somaliland—an Italian nun working at a Mogadishu children's hospital would be killed in 2006, a week after Pope Benedict made controversial comments about Islam during a lecture at the University of Regensburg. These were not natural targets, even in the violence-prone country. In 2003, Somaliland was being infiltrated by militants who took their inspiration from the bloody conflict in Iraq. Hargeisa did its best to crack down on the Islamists. Godane left that year, eluding the security forces, traveling south where he linked up with the Shabab. Five years later, in 2008, he would become their amir, and endeavor to re-open a front in his native Somaliland.

The fiery military leaders of the Shabab were balanced by more tempered clerics, who often presented themselves as "spokesmen" for the movement. In fact, the division of labor between the proclaimed military commanders—the amirs—and the spokesmen seems contrived. Rather than a unified group, with a division of tasks and tested structures of loyalty and authority, Al-Shabab has been an odd assemblage of clan militias and local business interests augmented by foreign jihadists. The amirs, based in Mogadishu, had embraced the global jihad paradigm of an all-out war. With connections to the foreign jihadists, comfortable with executing operations abroad, they wanted to open new fronts in Puntland and Somaliland. The other leaders riding with the Shabab remained grounded in the reality of their clan's best interests.

The movement has been in fact an alliance of autonomous regional operations. The southern port of Kismayo, in the South Juba province, had passed under the control of Shaykh Hassan Abdillahi Hersi ("Al-Turki"). A lieutenant of Aweys, a veteran of the Ogaden War and of Al-Ittihad, Al-Turki was in charge of Al-Shabab it its early days, when it was still the youth movement of the Islamic courts. After the Ethiopian invasion of 2006, he had first followed Aweys in the Hizbul Islam, and eventually rallied the new, more radical Al-Shabab. But Al-Turki was less defined by his shifting alliances than by his power base in Kismayo, where he has imposed Shariah. Shaykh Mukhtar Robow's ("Abu Mansur") power base was in the province around Baidoa. Robow came from the Shariah courts, and while his clerical background is well established, his credentials as a mujahideen are more opaque. He is sometimes said to have fought in Afghanistan under the Taliban, and to be connected with Saudi foundations once deeply involved in supporting the mujahideen milieu. But Robow was foremost a clan-based, religious leader. Robow presented himself as the spokesman of the Shabab until May 2009, when he publicly passed the torch to Shaykh Ali "Dheere," the conservative cleric who became famous as a court leader in Mogadishu in the mid-1990s.

The leaders' profiles open a window on the nature of the Shabab. The common denominator of these men is their fundamentalism, but while some have connections to the global jihadist currents outside Somalia, whether in Pakistan-Afghanistan or in the Arabian Peninsula, that is not the case of all. Their clan background is also diverse. Dheere hails from the Murusade-Hawiye, Godane from the Isaaq, Ayro from a subclan of the Habar Gidir-Hawiye, Robow from the Rahanweyn clan, and Al-Turki from the Darood-Ogaden. This apparent diversity masks more complicated divisions. At one level, the Shabab bring together individuals of various origins, driven by a common, belligerent opposition to the Transitional Government. At the same time, the Shabab have not fully transcended clan affiliations, but have simply federated different clan-based militias. Members of the Rahanweyn and Hawiye clans are numerically dominant among the rank and file by virtue of their being the majority in south Somalia.

When Sharif Ahmed returned to Somalia's capital in January 2009, the newly appointed president found himself holed up in south Mogadishu, with only Ugandan peacekeepers standing between his internationally recognized government and the Shabab, which controlled most of the city. The Shabab targeted high government officials with suicide attacks: in June 2009, thirty-five perished in the Hotel Medina in Beledweyne, when a minister was killed, and in December 2009, 25 more were killed, including three ministers, in the bombing of Hotel Shamo in Mogadishu.

Two French agents were captured in downtown Mogadishu in July 2009. One of them was released a month later by Aweys' Hizbul Islam; the other remained in the custody of the Shabab. France said the team was training Somali security forces: the international community had wished for a new Somali national army (to fight the Shabab) and navy (to fight the pirates), but both had difficulties getting off the ground. In June 2011, the Interior Minister of the Transitional Government was killed in another suicide attack in Mogadischu.

The decision in 2006 to back the Transitional Government and then the Ethiopian invasion had been a gamble for Washington, and many criticized the United States for destabilizing Somalia at a time when the Courts Union was restoring a form of order. The United States had been drawn into that war by the presence of operatives indicted for the 1998 embassy attacks in the company of the Somali militias affiliated with the Islamic Courts. But their eventual death was a pyrrhic victory. The chaos unleashed by the events of 2006–2007, and the terrorist risks the Shabab could now present beyond the borders of Somalia, compelled Washington to remain involved in the failed state with no endgame in sight. Young Americans of Somali descent were being recruited in the United States to join the jihad. The numbers were small—some twenty to thirty candidates, mostly from Minnesota—but some drew the short stick of suicide bombing missions. In both Europe and the United States, young citizens of Somali origin were affected by the violence in their ancestral land and began to dream up jihadist fantasies. Those who did not make it to Africa were picked up by law enforcement agencies and charged in terrorist conspiracies, their lives over before they started.

Besides Godane, the amir of the Shabab, radicals like Fuad Shongole in Mogadishu and Ibrahim Haji Jama ("Al-Afghani") in Kismayo had fully embraced the paradigm of a global jihad and served as points of contact for foreign jihadists—not just Americans and Europeans of Somali origin, but non-ethnic Somalis as well, possibly in the low hundreds. Omar Hammami ("Abu Mansur al-Amriki"), an American citizen of mixed Syrian heritage who was born in 1984 in Alabama, emerged in Somalia around 2007, making recruiting videos to the beat of jihadist rap. Terrorist attacks, car bombings, and suicide bombings were part of their arsenal—it was the foreigners who carried out the suicide missions. The conflict in Iraq had cooled down after 2007, and it became difficult for outsiders to move around there undetected. The Afghanistan-Pakistan front was active, but local. The various clusters of Taliban fighters were Pushtun and Pakistan had made it a point not to let outsiders back in the region. The death of Osama bin Laden in May 2011 only made clearer the point that the original branch of Al Qaeda had lost its bite. That made Somalia and Yemen the two most promising fronts for global jihadists. Weak states, long maritime borders with access to the sea, the proximity of financial and commercial centers like Mombasa and Dubai, the support of Eritrea and of conservative milieus in Saudi Arabia, and an abundance of small arms and explosives made the Bab el-Mandeb prime territory for jihad. By early 2010, a year after Sharif Sheikh Ahmed had assumed the presidency, the Shabab were referring publicly to Al Qaeda, claiming the brand as their own.

Embracing global jihadist paradigms meant the Shabab would not be content with a haven in south Somalia. Somali radicals had for a while been trying to breach into the north. There had been killings in Ethiopia-friendly Somaliland since 2001, an alluring target because of its border with Djibouti, host to French and American bases. An attack against foreign forces in the small country was a recurrent ambition for global jihadists. In 2008, violence broke out on a larger scale in the breakaway provinces of Puntland and Somaliland—a new operational direction imposed by Godane and Shongole. Ethiopian consulates, United Nations and African Union facilities were bombed and local leaders were assassinated. The simultaneous suicide attacks, carried out by infiltrated foreign jihadists, bore the signature of global jihad.

Then, in July 2010 the Shabab claimed responsibility for multiple, simultaneous bombings in Kampala, Uganda, that killed over seventy people watching the finals of the soccer World Cup. The justification for the bloody attack was the protection Ugandan forces provided to the Transitional Federal Government in Mogadishu. Somalia has been at war with Ethiopia in one form or another since the 1970s and been torn by factious disputes for decades, but by 2010 violence seemed to be finally seeping out of the local theater of operations. A faction of the Shabab was looking to build networks in other countries, and foreign militants were looking to enter Somalia for a chance to live the jihadist adventure, either in the south alongside the Shabab or in the new fronts in Puntland and Somaliland. As Yemen edged toward civil war in the summer of 2011, Washington worried the Somali Shabab would come together with the Yemeni jihadists, forming a new front straddling both sides of the Bab el-Mandeb and bent on attacking the American homeland. A Somali Shabab of secondary importance, Ahmed Abdulkadir Warsame, was captured at sea in April 2011 and brought to trial in New York with much fanfare by the Obama administration. He was presented as the link between the Yemeni and Somali jihadists.

In the same way that the United States had backed new regimes in Iraq and in Afghanistan to contain the local radicals, Washington now felt compelled to support the Transitional Government of Somalia until it was capable of taking on the Shabab on its own. Eventual success depended on the actual strength and cohesion of both sides, which was difficult to estimate.

The Shabab had imposed themselves over most of southern Somalia through a fundamentalist form of state terror. Their very brutality must have been compelling in the atmosphere of emergency created by the Ethiopian occupation. The Shabab then must have seemed relentless and capable. They knew that the strand of militant fundamentalism pioneered by the Wahhabis is a powerful instrument of social control: the Al-Sauds built a state around it. But it also has its drawbacks and limitations. Expansion through force works when force provides predictable security and gives access to increased resources, at the very least to loot that can be redistributed. In Somalia, it was one thing to navigate a society traumatized by the Ethiopian occupation, but the Shabab didn't have the ingredient that had made the earlier success of the Shariah courts: the ability to restore a modicum of prosperity through the imposition of order. Somalia is not Afghanistan, where the Taliban can count on the proceeds of a lucrative opium trade to buy allegiances. The Shabab had not been involved in the piratical ventures, in part because it was not their style and they did not have the skills. Toward the end of 2010 there were reports of a recreational yacht from South Africa beached in Baraawe, a small coastal town between Marka and Kismayo controlled by the Shabab, but that was an exception. The pirates' lairs were further north, beyond their reach. By 2011, the Shabab had yet to make a move into piracy or drug trafficking to build a consistent revenue stream.

The Shabab offered little in terms of social services to make their brutality palatable. They imposed on the population through what they called a *jaysh al-Hisbah*, an army to "combat vice and propagate virtue," that is, the classic religious police of salafis and Wahhabis. The Shabab fly an imposing black banner—the pledge to Islam in white Arabic script against a black background. Their strict salafi orthopraxy shuns music, has women veiled and men unshaven, and endorses the brutal public punishments of the hudud. Deviants are flogged or stoned, or have their limbs amputated. Girls are deterred from pursuing an education—in a country where almost half the population is illiterate. The epitome of cruelty may have been reached on October 27, 2008, when militiamen in Kismayo stoned to death a 13-year-old girl who had reported being raped by three men. Women were often the victims of those public displays of power, and it was common to force neighbors from their homes to witness the executions. The Shabab demanded more from the population than a passive audience to their zealotry. They levied a money and a blood tax. Payments had to be made at roadblocks. Boys attending Quranic schools were socialized in the fundamentalist milieu and sometimes forcibly inducted into the militia. The Shabab have operated openly, acting as the local government, holding frequent media conferences. Although they are intolerant of criticism, which they view as blasphemy and treason, they were unable to prevent tech-savvy Somalis from reporting to the wider world on the bleak local circumstances.

By 2010, a year after Sharif Ahmed took office, the Shabab were in control of the capital and most of Somalia south of Mogadishu. They faced more difficulty north of the capital, where their brand of Islam was met with fierce resistance. Salafis and Sufis have rarely been good companions, especially when salafis behave like hooligans, desecrating the tombs of revered Sufi saints and assassinating Sufi clerics. In the Galguduud province, Sufi orders and leaders of the local Habar Gidir and Marehan clans came together for protection. The new alliance, named Ahlu Sunnah wal-Jama'a ("the Path of Tradition and Community"), engaged the Shabab militarily and drove them out of the province. Ahlu Sunnah grew into a force to be reckoned with and spread to other areas, even repelling the Shabab from a section of Mogadishu, a feat that had eluded the official government, hemmed in by the jihadists. Farther north, in Hobyo, local clerics made accommodations with the pirates to put together a force capable of resisting the Shabab.

The Transitional Federal Government benefited from the brutality of its radical opponents, from their drift into global adventurism, and from its own access to foreign aid. The population had grown resentful over the loss of humanitarian assistance, an essential source of revenue in the poor country. Several leaders of the Ahlu Sunnah—the Sufi militia that stood against the Shabab—accepted ministerial posts. Yusuf Siad Inda'ade, the warlord who had become No. 3 in the Islamic Courts Union in 2006, had first thrown his lot with Aweys' Hizbul Islam, but eventually defected to become defense minister in Sharif Ahmed's Transitional Federal Government. The coalitional nature of the government is as much a sign of success as it is a weakness: ministries are fiefs run by autonomous warlords rather than pieces of a cohesive government. Politics in Somalia is opportunistic and mercenary; betrayal is a fact of life.

Aweys' Hizbul Islam had clashed with the Shabab on several occasions and cooperated on others. In December 2010, watching his movement marginalized, Aweys announced that the Hizbul Islam was now allied with the Shabab. That clarified the position of Eritrea, which was suspected of having been in some form or another behind both movements from the start. The Hizbul Islam had a different clan DNA, rooted in the Darood, and Aweys clan base in Central Somalia put him in charge of the front against Ahlu Sunnah wal-Jama'a. The rallying of Aweys came along with a leadership change in Al-Shabab, with ultraradical Godane being eclipsed by Ibrahim Haji Jama Mee'Add ("Al-Afghani"). An Isaaq from Somaliland, Al-Afghani had been involved in the Shabab operations in Kismayo, and his bid to leadership is said to have received support from Robow, who controlled the Baidoa region. The southern leaders of Al-Shabab seemed to be gaining the upper hand over the radicals in Mogadishu. Aversion for all things foreign was a trait of global jihadists not shared by all parties within the movement, and clan leaders who may have opportunistically ridden with Al-Shabab began to question the wisdom of chasing away foreign aid workers. When severe droughts hit south Somalia in the summer of 2011, leaving millions with scarce food supplies, political stances against foreign aid became untenable. To escape famine, thousands in Shabab-controlled areas marched south to the already overpopulated Kenyan refugee camp of Dadaab, the most vulnerable dying en route. Dadaab is a vast operation, the world's largest refugee complex. Three camps in Ethiopia were open to Somali refugees, as were camps and distribution centers in government-controlled areas.

The ordeal was the opportunity for the Transitional Federal Government to shine, which was easier said than done given the lack of discipline of its soldiers. In any case, pictures of starving Somali children circulated around the world were an indictment for the Shabab. Their religious utopia had nothing to offer against malnutrition: aid from the World Food Program and medical care was on the other side, with the government. By July, commanders in the Baidoa region reversed their position and allowed UNICEF to airlift food there. Around Mogadishu, Shabab commanders were reported regrouping people to prevent them from crossing over to government-controlled areas. The humanitarian crisis turned into a strategic disaster, and on August 6, Shabab militias withdrew from the Somali capital.

The Shabab had stormed southern Somalia, but after four years of terror, the phenomenon was overstretched, simultaneously taking on Sufis, moderate Islamists, the international donors' community, and the well-organized forces of the autonomous provinces of Puntland and Somaliland. Moreover, the Al Qaeda brand they claimed was tainted, sure to attract American hostility and be strategically self-defeating in the long run. The more the Shabab kept up their apocalyptic run, the more likely they were to self-destruct. Somali clan leaders are opportunist survivors. As had been the case in similar conflicts—in Bosnia, Chechnya, and Iraq—the interests of global jihadists and local Islamists are rarely aligned for long.

The new government in Somalia may be militarily inept and may remain weak for a while, but as long as there is cash to spare, it may have the momentum of seduction on its side. The key to the future is the flow of foreign aid and the balance of power between Ethiopia, which has friends in various militias north of Mogadishu, and Eritrea, which is widely seen as the backer of the factions that prevail south of the capital.

CHAPTER SEVEN

Al Qaeda Redux

THE THIRD ACT OF AL QAEDA in Yemen opened on a dramatic prison break. In February 2006, 23 men escaped from the basement of the Political Security Office, the Yemeni agency for domestic intelligence, in downtown Sanaa. A 140-meter-long tunnel had been dug between the prison and a washroom in a nearby mosque, possibly from both ends. It is believed that the guards had turned a blind eye. One of those men, Jamal al-Badawi, had escaped from death row once before, in 2003, with the alleged complicity of a colonel in the security organization. In addition to his proficiency as an escape artist, Al-Badawi was known for being the man who had sent the two suicide bombers on their fatal mission against the *USS Cole* in 2000. Another escapee was involved in the bombing of the *Limburg* tanker. All 23 were Islamist militants.

The relationship between the Yemeni government and the jihadists went back to the 1990s. Mujahideen fresh from Afghanistan had fought on the side of Sanaa against the socialist, secessionist government in Aden during the 1994 civil war. Thereafter, a "live and let live" arrangement prevailed between President Saleh and the jihadists, who were left alone as long as they did not interfere with his regime. The 2000 operation against the *USS Cole* had brought unwelcome attention to Yemen, and the government had had to balance mollifying Washington with preserving the pact with the radicals. Things went from bad to worse with the 2001 attacks against the United States. Saleh made a point of going to Washington that winter to show support for the War on Terror. The U.S. offered military aid and training for a Yemeni counterterrorism unit. The price was to go after the Al Qaeda men implicated in the *USS Cole* and *Limburg* attacks who were still at large in Yemeni territory.

Washington was after two operatives in particular: Ali Qaed Senyan al-Harthi, a Yemeni and at the time the highest-ranking Al Qaeda member in Yemen, and Mohammed Hamdi al-Ahdil, a Saudi. The two men had sought refuge in Al-Hosun, a small village in the Ma'rib province, paying rent to the local tribesmen. A government raid on the village in December 2001 had left eighteen soldiers and six villagers dead, but the two jihadists had decamped long before the assault. The government arrested the local shaykhs and kept their sons hostage in return for information on the fugitives. This episode is not a statement on the local sympathy for Al Qaeda, but rather an illustration of the tension between the tribes and the regime. Ma'rib is the principal oil-producing province in Yemen, yet its inhabitants have seen little of that rent, and government men are bad news.

The two jihadists had disappeared in the desert. Al-Harthi was killed in a CIA drone attack in October the following year. The Yemeni counterterrorism unit had better luck with Al-Ahdil the second time around, capturing him in November 2003. Saleh was keeping the promise made in Washington to clamp down on Al Qaeda elements. But back home, accommodations were made and sentences were reduced. Al-Ahdil would serve a three-year sentence. Jamal al-Badawi, the field commander of the *USS Cole* cell who had been condemned to death and had twice escaped, was finally pardoned after turning himself in to the Yemeni authorities. The government of Yemen was hoping to preserve the relationship with Washington and the arrangement with the jihadists. It hoped to reap the benefits of being neutral ground, but none of the parties in that war had much interest in neutral grounds.

The map of global jihad had changed considerably after 2001. The loss of the Afghan sanctuary following the U.S.-led invasion had driven Saudi jihadists to move the fight back home. In the small world of Al Qaeda, the task of building an operational base in the kingdom rested on two men. The first was Abd al-Rahim al-Nashiri, the head of the cell responsible for the *USS Cole* and the *Limburg* naval attacks—the man who had called Al-Badawi from the United Arab Emirates and ordered the attack against American destroyer. But Al-Nashiri was arrested in late 2002 in the United Arab Emirates. That left Yusuf al-Uyayri to do the job. According to Thomas Hegghammer, Al-Uyayri was a Qasimi from Burayda, in the historical heartland of Wahhabism. His pedigree gave him access to the most conservative Nejdis. Besides setting up an operational network in Riyadh within a short period of time, Al-Uyayri produced a vast amount of instructional material for prospective jihadists, including online videos and publications addressing topics such as the permissibility of martyrdom operations (suicide bombings) and of executing captives.

At the same time Al-Uyayri was building operational assets in Riyadh, Saudi Arabia had come under scrutiny from the United States. After all, fifteen of the nineteen 9/11 hijackers hailed from the kingdom. Tension between the two allies would only grow after the U.S.-led overthrow of the Iraqi Baathist regime in 2003. The Iraq campaign stirred discontent throughout the region and justified a human traffic of jihadist and shahid ("martyr") wannabes coalescing in Syria before crossing into Iraq to fight the infidels. Local handlers were prompt at preparing and sending them on suicide missions against American forces. Either for money or for glory, young Saudis and Yemenis joined their ranks. The Saudi government, tethered to its long-standing security relationship with the United States, could no longer deny that it was home to anti-American radicals.

It all came to a boil in the spring of 2003. A safe house was discovered in March in Riyadh, exposing for the first time the existence of an operational network in the Saudi capital. It was one thing for the Saudi regime to shrug at terror abroad but quite another to endure it at home, and it pursued that trail without mercy. Pressured, the jihadists responded in May with multiple attacks involving gunmen and suicide bombers against Western expatriates housed in residential compounds in Riyadh. During the months that followed, the kingdom was engulfed in a wave of violence targeting expatriates, security forces, and oil facilities. There was another large attack against a residential compound in November 2003. Paul Johnson, an American engineer, was abducted in 2004 and beheaded in June. His ordeal was carefully staged over the weeks, and his execution broadcast on the Internet. Snuff films are a particularly extreme type of propaganda that originated in Chechnya. They have been used only by the most radical elements of the global jihad movement, in Pakistan (where an American journalist met this fate) and in Iraq (where the group led by Al-Zarqawi produced several snuff videos).

The violence in Riyadh was testimony to the progress and efficiency of the Saudi security apparatus—which could count on the discreet help of FBI forensic investigators. This was not 1979, when commandos from the French counter-terrorism unit found the Saudis unprepared to handle the hostage crisis then unfolding in the Grand Mosque of Mecca. The Saudi regime had had two decades to build up its security forces, and as they swept through the fundamentalist milieus, jihadist cells came out for last-stand, suicide operations. By the end of 2004, the operational ability of Al Qaeda in Saudi Arabia was all but nil. Yusuf al-Uyayri, the man who had set up the structure in Riyadh, had perished in a shootout in May 2003. Each subsequent operation killed more jihadists. The least committed and least compromised turned themselves in. They were enrolled in a deradicalization program. Others left for friendlier skies, but habitats that could accommodate jihadists were rapidly shrinking. By 2006, the popular mood in Iraq was turning against foreign militants who had brought nothing but bloodshed, and the surge of American troops made it imprudent to move there. Suddenly, Yemen beckoned from across a long, porous border.

One man who made it to Yemen was Said Ali al-Shihri. Al-Shihri, a Saudi born in 1973, was captured in December 2001 trying to cross from Afghanistan into Pakistan. He was found to be a "travel facilitator" for Al Qaeda, arranging trips from Bahrain to Afghanistan via Iran. Held in Guantanamo for six years, he was released in November 2007 to Saudi authorities to be enrolled in a rehabilitation and reintegration program. But Al-Shihri graduated from his experiences a more radical man, and after just a few months he crossed into Yemen to join fellow jihadists. He was not alone. Mohammed Al-Owfi, another Saudi, followed the same path from Guantanamo to the Saudi rehabilitation program to Yemen. Their cases became public after they posed in provocative videos posted online. They had apparently risen to leadership positions in the Yemen-based group.

Those cases shed a negative light on the Saudi deradicalization program, but the results have been satisfactory overall. Saudi Arabia has estimated that of 270 militants to have undergone the program as of 2010, only eleven joined Al Qaeda in Yemen—all of them ex-Guantanamo detainees. Life as a jihadist in Yemen must not have been all that they had hoped for: a couple turned themselves back in to Saudi authorities. Remarkably, Al-Owfi, who at one point appeared to be No. 4 in the chain of command of the jihadist group, was among the two defectors. He would be back in Saudi Arabia in February 2009, making claims that Al Qaeda militants in Yemen were financed by Libya and Iran. The Saudi government diplomatically eliminated those statements from the record, but not until after they had been reported by the media.

By 2008, the cat was out of the bag: Yemen was now a hotbed of global jihadists. The big man, the "amir" of what had yet to become Al Qaeda in the Arabian Peninsula, was Nasr al-Wuhayshi. Al-Wuhayshi, a native Yemeni, had served as secretary to Bin Laden in Afghanistan, which he had left in late 2001. Arrested while crossing into Iran, he had been deported to and incarcerated in Yemen. He was one of the twenty-three men who escaped in the 2006 prison break. Al-Wuhayshi, along with fellow escapee Qasim al-Raymi, would be the backbone of the Al Qaeda cell in Yemen. Al-Raymi was a younger man, born in 1979, who would carry out the dirty work of operational commander and second-in-command to Al-Wuhaysi until his death by air strike in January 2010. Al-Shihri, the Saudi runaway, allegedly became No. 3 in the organization.

Yemen was not a natural battleground for global jihadists. There are no Western troops, no Christian (or Jewish) power sitting on Muslim lands, and no army of foreign contractors and expatriates working for the regime. Yemen does not even have the sprawling seaside resorts of Taba and Sharm el-Sheikh, Egyptian symbols of Westernized decadence that have been targeted by their ilk. Even Dubai and its showy extravagance would have made a more natural target, but Dubai has managed to always be on the good side of the jihadists. Yemen's sparse tourists, drawn to the unique architecture and surreal landscapes of this ancient country, would make for poor targets. But what Yemen offered was a mountainous terrain, scattered settlements, and gaps in security that gave militants the space to operate.

The jihadists followed the path of least resistance: they kept a light footprint in the cities and stayed away from the Zaidi Shias. They settled among the eastern tribes in remote, mountainous rural areas of the Jawf, Ma'rib, Shabwa, and Abyan provinces: a north-south axis east of the capital, in the highlands running from the Saudi border to the Arabian Sea. It helped that some of the militants were originally from the area. Robert Worth tells how Fahd al-Quso, a Yemeni wanted in relation to the USS Cole bombing, was instrumental in building relationships between the jihadists and a tribe in the Rafadh Valley in the Shabwa province. His family was originally from that valley. He paid for schoolteachers to come to a village the government had neglected for years. It was not more ideological than that.

The social situation in Yemen was propitious. A little money could go far in building bridges with tribes cut off from government patronage and alienated by the regime. Those tribes were well-armed and battle-tested, having a history of internecine hostility which, too, could be leveraged. The economic hardships of a young population offered ample opportunities to lure gunmen with a few hundred dollars and an appeal to honor and tradition.

Yemen is the Arab nation that sent the most mujahideen to Afghanistan in the 1980s, its contingent in the thousands and second only to that of Pakistan. Many went for the money.

At the same time, lack of education and traditional forms of social relations limit the degree to which rural Yemenis can be mobilized. A student away from home or a migrant worker may embrace a new ideology and affiliation, discarding all previous forms of identification and socialization. But if a tribal group does business with a jihadist movement, it will do so within the constraints of traditional patterns of exchange, maintaining its autonomy as a tribe. At some point, the tribal group of the recruits is bound to resent being drained of its young, especially if it is clear that jihad is a one-way trip to death. Tribes are better armed than the jihadists, with an abundance of AK-47s and rocket-propelled grenades. The jihadists cannot intimidate Yemeni tribes; they can only incentivize.

Finally, jihadists could expect some sympathy, if not actual support, from the followers of Shaykh al-Zindani. The salafis were established in the cities and, like the jihadists, consumed by anti-Americanism. Yemen was a fallback plan now that Saudi Arabia was lost, but not a terrible one. The killings began without glory. In July 2007, a suicide bomber drove into a group of Spanish tourists at the Balkis temple in the Ma'rib province. In January 2008, Belgian tourists were gunned down in a valley in the Hadramawt. In March 2009, South Korean tourists were killed by a bomb, watching the sunset over the ancient city of Shibam in the

Hadramawt. There also were attacks against government outposts, oil facilities, state security personnel, and foreign embassy workers in Sanaa. But a handful of tourists here and there could not hurt a tourism sector that had long been in sufferance.

The new group kept alive the original hope of Al Qaeda to provoke the United States into a big confrontation. In March 2008, they fired mortar rounds at the U.S. Embassy in Sanaa, only to hit a girls school nearby. In September, they went back at it with an ambitious coordinated assault, throwing everything at the American compound: car bombs and rocket-propelled grenades and volleys from automatic rifles. They failed to breach the walls. This was not Beirut in 1983, when the American Embassy there was blown up twice in two years, or Islamabad, where it was torched to the ground by an angry crowd of Islamists. The world had changed on Al Qaeda. American Embassies in the Muslim world were unassailable compounds, and U.S. destroyers would no longer let a small skiff approach them. The group had to take stock of its operational limitations and get imaginative.

There were other ways to get attention. Like other ji-hadist groups, it knew that one way to break through on the world stage was to claim the Al Qaeda brand, which it did loudly and publicly in January 2009. The Yemen group was now called Al Qaeda in the Arabian Peninsula. But even before then, the group had taken the art of jihadist public relations to new heights. In 2008 it started publishing an online magazine, *Sada al-Malahim* (the "Echo of

Battles"). Its pages provide an alternative reading of political developments in the region, with hyperbolic reports on the successes of jihadist fighters to attract recruits. Young Muslim men with no previous record of religiosity and militancy are bound to encounter the jihadist narrative. Life in their home country was what it was: some had opportunities, others faced a bleak future. Domestic media were patently unreliable mouthpieces for the regimes, and what they had to say about jihad and the jihadists could not be trusted. And so when Al Qaeda in the Arabian Peninsula portrayed armed struggle as a successful and empowering alternative to a drab existence, there was little against which to judge the kind of truth it peddled. Feelings of fraternal victimization and outrage were nourished by well-crafted propaganda that used the abundant footage of violence in Muslim lands. There was a motive—deprivation and victimization—and there was a means—jihad—to correct it. The gap between the reality of jihad (death or capture in a more or less distant horizon) and the fantasy of jihad (redemption, salvation, empowerment, and success) was never contemplated until too late. The machine churned its harvest of recruits, which were few in numbers but sufficient to keep the embers of armed struggle alive.

In the summer of 2010, the Yemeni group started an English-language publication called *Inspire*, possibly authored and edited by Samir Khan, an American blogger of Pakistani descent. Born in Saudi Arabia in 1986, Khan had lived in North Carolina and Queens, New York, and had been a prolific online supporter of the jihadist creed from his late teens. He moved to Yemen to study Arabic. The new magazine was a recruiting, legitimizing, and fundraising instrument. It displayed good technical quality with colorful images and careful editing. It offered practical advice, such as ways to communicate online with fellow radicals without being detected by Western authorities. The genius of *Inspire* was that its first edition became an instant phenomenon, thanks in particular to an article about making bombs in your mother's kitchen. It was picked up by every news network around the world. The strategy to reach copycats by providing practical information about explosives would be pursued by Al Qaeda into late 2010, when it published the English-language *Explosives Course* on numerous websites.

The Yemeni group had gotten another break in November 2009, when Nidal Malik Hasan, a U.S. Army major of Palestinian origins, entered an Army medical facility and shot at the people assembled there. The facility was in Fort Hood, Texas, where Hasan worked as a psychiatrist. His connection to Yemen came from a few e-mails exchanged with an American imam based there, Anwar al-Awlaki. Al-Awlaki was born to Yemeni parents in 1971 in New Mexico. His father, a member of the powerful Awlaki tribe, was pursuing higher education in the United States. Anwar's family returned to Yemen in 1978, where his father reached prominent positions, for a time serving as minister of agriculture and later as president of Sana'a University.

The younger Al-Awlaki returned to the United States in 1991 to study civil engineering at Colorado State University. While in Denver he volunteered at a small local mosque. In 1994 he moved to San Diego, where he served in a couple of local mosques. Al-Awlaki's limited training in Islamic theology and jurisprudence was in keeping with the practice of the new Islamism. The conviction that official ulema were corrupt and compromised by their allegiance to the rulers legitimized a younger breed of activists who interpreted the faith in the light of novel needs. In the West, where Muslim communities were recent and mosques few and far between, the willingness to volunteer more than made up for the lack of credentials. It was while serving as imam in a San Diego mosque that Al-Awlaki met two of the future 9/11 hijackers. In 2000 he left San Diego and moved to Falls Church, Virginia, where he worked at the Dar al-Hijrah Islamic Center, a renowned institution in the Muslim Brotherhood tradition. His position got him invited to the Pentagon during outreach luncheons. His sermons throughout those years in the United States, even after the 9/11 attacks, stopped short of advocating violence. He was fundamentalist and militant, a fiery advocate for Muslim rights in the United States, but he remained within the bounds of the law of the land.

In late 2001, Al-Awlaki was questioned on several occasions by the FBI in relation to his connection with participants in the 9/11 attacks, which may have prompted him to leave for the United Kingdom in early 2002. He finally returned to Yemen in 2004, where he became involved in online Islamic counseling, a growing business that links Muslims isolated in the diaspora with Islamic clerics who can guide them in the ways of the faith. The most famous of these sites is probably islamonline.net, which is associated with the prominent Egyptian Shaykh Yusuf al-Qaradawi. If Al-Awlaki's theological credentials were lacking, he made up for it with his command of English, which enabled him to relate to Muslims for whom this was the first and only language.

From Yemen, Al-Awlaki's statements turned virulently critical of the United States' policies toward Muslim countries (Iraq and Afghanistan, but also Somalia and Yemen), and he became an advocate of armed struggle in the defense of Islam. At the behest of the United States, he was detained by the Yemeni government in 2006 and 2007. It is after that experience that Al-Awlaki's online activity put him in contact with Hasan, the Fort Hood shooter. Al-Awlaki was not alone in preaching jihad on the Web, and the few e-mails the two men exchanged may have been ancillary to Hasan's decision to shoot his colleagues. But the incident had drawn attention to Al-Awlaki, and beyond him to the group of jihadists in Yemen. Suddenly, Al-Awlaki appeared to be the ultimate weapon. He did not need to cross borders; he did not need to get close to its targets. It was the fatwa against Salman Rushdie all over again. Al-Awlaki, it was feared, could get into the mind of any American Muslim and turn him against his compatriots.

The United States had been surprisingly spared of copycats following 9/11, but things suddenly changed. The Fort Hood shooting coincided with the arrest of a young Afghan, Najibullah Zazi, who, while a resident in the United States, was planning suicide bombings in the New York subway in the fall of 2009. A few months later, in May 2010, a young

American of Pakistani origin, Faisal Shahzad, left in Times Square a vehicle loaded with explosives that failed to detonate. After his arrest, Shahzad mentioned Al-Awlaki as a source of inspiration. That same month Roshonara Choudhry, a 21-year old-British woman of Bengali background who had been listening to Al-Awlaki's sermons online, stabbed a former Labor minister. The scare of domestic sleeper cells ran through the media for a while, but in the end amounted to little. Al-Awlaki spoke good English, but he could not change the fact that the vast majority of Muslims living in the West were busy with their jobs and their families and had no time for jihad.

The third accomplishment that should be credited to the Yemeni group is the invention of new ways to deliver explosive charges. Exhibit one is what has been called the crotch bomb, an undergarment variation on the vest bomb, which is filled with pentaerythritol tetranitrate. In September 2009, this contraption allowed a militant to bring explosive material into the office of Prince Mohammed bin Nayef, the son of the Interior minister and head of Saudi counterterrorism. The bomb was carried by Abdullah Hasan al-Asiri, a Saudi member of the jihadist group who had returned in pretense to surrender in person to the prince. The prince survived.

The same trick eluded security at Amsterdam Schiphol Airport on Christmas Day 2009. Umar Farouk Abdulmutallab, an upper-class Nigerian educated in London, tried but failed to detonate his device on a Northwest Airlines flight to Detroit. He survived to reveal that the operation had been hatched in Yemen. The young man had first been there in 2004–2005, studying at the Iman University affiliated with Al-Zindani and the salafist movement. He had returned in the summer of 2009, which is probably when he was recruited and trained for the mission and at which time he said he had been in contact with Al-Awlaki. The son of a minister had prepped the son of a banker for his suicide mission. Despite the operational failure, Al Qaeda in the Arabian Peninsula was happy to claim responsibility for the attack in retaliation for a recent U.S. drone attack in Yemen.

In November 2010, the same explosive would find its way inside toner cartridges shipped through two different air couriers to Chicago. The bombs were designed to explode in flight and take down the planes. The plot was reportedly foiled after a man named Jabir al-Fayfi informed his Saudi handlers of what was unfolding. Al-Fayfi was a former jihadist, interned in Guantanamo and released to Saudi authorities. He was rehabilitated through the Saudi deradicalization program and then infiltrated Al Qaeda in the Arabian Peninsula as a double agent. Rehabilitation failures, it turns out, are not what they seem to be. In the battle between Saudi officials and Saudi radicals, deception applies across the board.

The man credited with this creative activity is Ibrahim Hassan al-Asiri, the older brother of the suicide bomber who tried to kill Prince Mohammed bin Nayef. Al-Asiri was born in 1982, the son of a Saudi military man. Ordinary in many ways, he reportedly was not religious until the age of

18, a pattern that, too, is ordinary. He was arrested by Saudi authorities while trying to enter illegally into Iraq to join the jihadists. He was later released, and he and his brother disappeared in 2007, when they joined the group in Yemen.

The first incarnation of Al Qaeda, in the days of Khalid Sheikh Mohammed, did not claim responsibility for its operations. They were so spectacular, in design if not execution, that they were meant to speak for themselves. But Al Qaeda in the Arabian Peninsula was less fastidious—and less successful. It ran a small operation on a low budget: a daytime raid on a bank truck in downtown Aden in August 2009 allegedly yielded 1 million rials (about $500,000). The group understood the value of publicity and rushed to claim responsibility—even for its failures. In psychological warfare, perception is what matters and those men were drawing attention to themselves with highly visible if overly ambitious operations. They did not have to succeed: they needed only to make themselves known and the reputation of Al Qaeda would do the rest, triggering an aversive response from a collective psyche still deeply marked by the events of 9/11.

The rise of Al Qaeda in the Arabian Peninsula and its global fame have been a challenge and a blessing for President Saleh. The threat of jihadists has brought Sanaa millions of dollars in U.S. economic and military aid since 2000—and the more visible Al Qaeda is, the greater the payoff, in the hundreds of millions of dollars in 2010. Yemen had acquired such notoriety that the international community had to commit to the preservation of the

regime, lest the alternative be another failed state on the
scale of Somalia or Afghanistan, where militants would run
wild. Western anxieties gave Saleh room to maneuver
against his most pressing enemies, which were not Al Qaeda
but the Zaidi Houthis and the secessionist Southern Movement. In fact, the Yemeni government was suspected of
portraying the casualties of clashes between secessionists
and the army as casualties of military operations against Al
Qaeda in the Arabian Peninsula, hyping the jihadist threat
to get more aid and less scrutiny.

The United States kept its eyes on the prey and prudently
avoided getting involved in partisan battles. Drone attacks
were conducted in tribal areas in December 2009 and May
2010 against militants related to the Al Qaeda group. The
death of civilians was built up to embarrass the regime, but
President Saleh remained committed to allowing American
aerial operations inside Yemen as long as financial support
was forthcoming. All it took was a bit of obfuscation: there
were discussions about replacing drone attacks with American air strikes that could be claimed by the Yemeni air force.
Saleh was reported saying to American Gen. David Petraeus
that he would "continue saying the bombs are ours, not
yours."

At the same time, the Yemeni government's soft approach
to the radicals had been one of the main obstacles to the
closing of the Guantanamo detention center, where the
largest group of prisoners that remained after ten years was
Yemeni. There were doubts in Washington that they could

be held in their home country and that the Yemeni rehabilitation program would be effective. The fate of Al-Awlaki was a dilemma for the regime. The American patrons wanted him killed, but he was the son of a relatively important man from a powerful tribe, and a selling point for more military aid. The Americans were not duped: diplomatic cables from the embassy in Sanaa reveal great lucidity about the way President Saleh was playing the game, and that every service or tolerance had to be paid with cash, weapons, or technical assistance.

Matters took a turn for the worse in late November 2010, when Al Qaeda in the Arabian Peninsula claimed responsibility for suicide truck bombings in the northern province of Jawf. The bombs had targeted Zaidi crowds assembled for a religious festival. Tension immediately flared between the Zaidi Houthi militias—who had earlier in the year conceded to a truce imposed by the Yemeni government—and the followers of local salafi clerics. The pretext for Al Qaeda was precisely the truce, as it exposed the failure of the government to eliminate the Zaidi "apostates." Until then, there had been several fields of contestation in Yemen, but all were independent of one another and the salafi movement, although ideologically related to the Al Qaeda phenomenon, had remained on the sidelines. The attack against Zaidi civilians aimed to ignite a direct sectarian conflagration between salafis and Zaidis, to rupture the bulkheads that had allowed Sanaa to keep the situation under control. Jihadists had attempted that strategy before, in Egypt by attacking the Copts and in Iraq by attacking the Shias.

It was one thing for Washington to pursue a handful of exiled Saudi jihadists in the mountains of central Yemen; quite another to get trapped in the middle of a civil war raging in a failed state. But by January 2011, history took an unexpected turn and the mischief of the local Al Qaeda was eclipsed by the popular protests that erupted throughout the country. The jihadists were resoundingly absent from the movement to overthrow Saleh, and the protesters, like their brethren in Egypt and Tunisia and Libya, showed no interest in the self-defeating ideology of a global jihad. The fall of Tunisia's Ben Ali and Egypt's Mubarak after a few weeks of non-violent political activism had made a mockery of jihadist tactics. The focus of the Yemeni protesters was on the corruption of the regime and the stunted opportunities they faced in an underdeveloped economy. The West was not really in their line of vision: if it was not going to help, at least it should not get in the way by siding with the status quo against the calls of the street.

Saleh had played the salafists to conquer the south culturally, and he had played the jihadists for foreign aid, which extended his lease on power. The troops that remained loyal to Saleh several months into the protests included the Special Forces and Counter-Terrorism units trained by the United States, and commanded by his son Ahmed and by his nephew Yahya. For Washington, the dilemma was whether to continue with military assistance amidst the wave of antiregime contestation. Ideological affinity dictated to back the young protesters, but their pristine political expression did not easily translate into a functional system of governance. With other two thirds of the Yemeni population still rural and tribal, the young urbanites who demanded unfettered democracy were unlikely to deliver the votes come election time. Washington's expectations for Yemen were limited to effective counterterrorism, and Saleh, for all his duplicity, had been the solution of expediency. The anti-Saleh camp, which had expanded to include the established political opposition, knew that, and it claimed to whoever would listen that with the *ancien régime* out of the way, Yemen's fortunes would immediately improve and the local Al Qaeda boys would be dealt with. But Western capitals, anxious about jihadists to the point of inhibition and incapable of deciphering Yemen's new political landscape, missed that rendezvous with history.

As the political crisis dragged on in the central cities of Taiz and Sanaa and the army split, violence flared up in the countryside from which troops were withdrawn. In April, a tribal militia in a southern village of the Lahej province attacked an encampment of Ahmed Saleh's Presidential Guards. In March, a group of Islamist fighters that called themselves Ansar al-Shariah had taken over the village of Jaar in the nearby Abyan province, and by May they were in control of the coastal provincial capital, Zinjibar. Their connection to Al Qaeda in the Arabian Peninsula remained uncertain—their numbers suggested a local, tribal dimension, but their ideology was unabashedly jihadist.

Concerned by those developments, the United States conducted drone attacks in the Abyan province in May and June, one of which targeted and missed Anwar al-Awlaki. Nothing could be done to restore order in Yemen in the short run, but the hope was to surgically remove the elements inclined to take violence overseas. There were drone attacks on the other side of the Bab al-Mandeb as well, and by the summer of 2011 Yemen and Somalia eerily mirrored each other. On both shores, a core of global jihadists was hosted by a force of tribal salafi militias running loose in a failed state. In Somalia, the Transitional Government of Sharif Ahmed was struggling to roll back the Shabab. In Yemen, an odd coalition of putative leaders—the renegade general Ali Mohsen, the former mujahideen turned spearhead of the secessionist Southern Movement Tariq al-Fadhli—were trying to formulate a plan to take back the Abyan province from the salafis. With the corpse of the Saleh regime still warm, their enthusiastic commitment to fight Al Qaeda and the runaway salafis was a petition for American support in the political transition.

In the end, Somalia would remain an Ethiopian problem and Yemen a Saudi problem. But the risk of even one successful transnational operation was one the Obama administration could not afford in the buildup to a Presidential election. In May 2011, the Yemeni jihadists had been the first to acknowledge that Osama Bin Laden had been killed, a deliberate visibility that established them as the last group capable of claiming the original mantle of Al Qaeda. There were other active global jihadists—for instance in the

Sahara—but those referred to Al Qaeda for publicity purposes, without serious commitment to its core transnational idea of attacking in the heart of the West. Al Qaeda in the Arabian Peninsula still hoped to be the real thing, but to succeed in this endeavor, it would have to take down a Western airliner. For all their structural limitations, that made the Yemeni radicals, and their potential allies in Somalia, Washington's number one counterterrorism problem.

CHAPTER EIGHT

The Sad Lands

O N FEBRUARY 3, 1976, a school bus was seized by militants from the Somali Coast Liberation Front. On board were 30 children of French military personnel stationed in Djibouti, which was known for years as the "French Coast of the Somalis." The bus was stopped just short of a border crossing, within the shooting range of sympathetic Somali border guards. The militants, ethnic Somalis from Djibouti, demanded independence from France and merger with the Republic of Somalia. The hostage crisis ended a day later when the militants were killed by snipers from the new unit of the French military specializing in counterterrorism and hostage rescue.

The Gulf of Tadjoura is a deep indentation inside the rocky, arid landscape of the Somali coast. On its southern shore lies Djibouti, the African port that sits immediately opposite the Arabian port of Aden. Together, Aden and Djibouti frame the Bab el-Mandeb, guarding access to the Red Sea. In 1862 the French obtained a lease on Obock, a small port on the north shore of the Gulf of Tadjoura. The French were moving along on the project to build a canal at Suez between the Mediterranean and the Red Seas. As part of the project, Obock was designed as a coaling station. But Djibouti, on the southern shore, was a better port, and the French colonial administration moved there in 1892. Eventually, the French would carve out a small, horseshoe-shaped protectorate around the Gulf of Tadjoura.

The "French Coast of the Somalis" was a misnomer. The north shore of the Gulf of Tadjoura was the land of Danakils, a redoubtable nomadic tribe that spoke the Afar language. Their homeland, the Dankali coast, is split into what today are north Djibouti, south Eritrea, and eastern Ethiopia. On the southern shore of the Gulf of Tadjoura live nomadic Somalis of the Issas clan. Both Danakils and Somalis are Muslims. Both Afar and Somali are Cushitic languages, related yet distinctive enough to maintain social divisions between the two groups. Both lived for 85 years under French administration.

The nationalist winds of the 1950s were blowing through Djibouti, and in 1958 the French authorities organized a referendum regarding the future of their protectorate. Many Somalis were evicted before the election, allowing the Danakils and the French residents of Djibouti to vote in favor of continued association with France. When the Republic of Somalia in the south became independent in 1960, Djibouti became the object of irredentist claims that in the mid-1970s turned to terrorism—including the 1976 hijacking of the school bus by the Somali Coast Liberation Front. France granted Djibouti independence in June 1977.

Djibouti would go through one civil war and two presidents during its first thirty-four years of sovereignty.

Hassan Gouled Aptidon, a Somali nationalist, was consistently reelected from 1977 to 1999. In 1991, an insurgent group recruiting primarily from the Danakil population rebelled against his essentially one-party regime and started a civil war that would sputter on until 2000. The frustrations were genuine, but combat operations were limited, which allowed the situation to improve incrementally throughout the 1990s. Rebel factions were integrated into a coalition government as the political system opened up to freer, multiparty elections. In 1999, an aging Aptidon was replaced by his nephew, head of security and Chief of Staff Ismail Omar Guelleh.

Guelleh was a classic African strongman. He started as a policeman and then had a stint as a noncommissioned officer, which was followed by a long career in intelligence and domestic security. Guelleh is Somali; the prime minister and foreign minister are Danakils. The reconciliation process after the civil war has made for a broad coalition government, but some Danakils are still suspicious of what they see as a structural bias toward Somalis. And the move toward more political participation receded after 2005. In 2010, Guelleh modified the constitution to be eligible for a third term. In April 2011, in the midst of the great Arab Spring, he was re-elected with 80% of the votes in a contest boycotted by the opposition. Opposition leaders had been arrested and international monitors had been expelled. This political and ethnic tension plays out in a small territory of 23,000 square kilometers (about 8,900 square miles), occupied by a population of just over

700,000, two-thirds of whom reside in the capital city of Djibouti.

Djibouti is the African mouth of the Great Rift Valley, which runs from northern Lebanon to Malawi. The environment is harsh and arid, a lunar landscape of dried lava under scorching heat that only ever allowed for low-density pastoralism. Salt is mined from Lake Assal, the hottest and lowest part of Africa at 155 meters below sea level. Djibouti's value and resources are not found in its forbidding environment but in its strategic location between the Red Sea and the Gulf of Aden. Djibouti's fortunes turned when the 1998 war between Ethiopia and Eritrea signified the indispensability of the small nation as an outlet for Ethiopian trade. An old French-era railroad linked the port of Djibouti to Addis Ababa, but fresh investments from Dubai vastly improved the transit facilities. Dubai Ports International obtained a twenty-year lease to operate the seaport. The emirati investors built a new terminal at the airport and a deep-sea port with an oil terminal and a free zone for foreign companies to set up local facilities under preferential conditions. No other regional port can compete with Djibouti's infrastructure.

Dubai has promised a lot to Djibouti: to turn the poor African nation into a thriving metropolis of industry and recreation. A hotel, villas, and apartments are to be built to kick-start local tourism. The partners got even more ambitious with a project for a 29-kilometer bridge across the Bab el-Mandeb. Tarek bin Laden, an investor based in Dubai and half-brother of Osama, has played a leading role in the bridge project. The family company, the Saudi Binladin Group, was enlisted to build new twin "Cities of Light"— Noor City—as bookends to the new bridge, one in Yemen, the other in Djibouti. Work on the bridge was begun in 2009, but stalled because of the financial crisis hitting Dubai investors. It is not clear what traffic can be realistically expected, but Dubai's investment strategy has always been to build first and worry later about luring investors and businesses.

In 2001, Djibouti leased a camp to the United States Navy, which passed under the control of the U.S. Africa Command formed soon after. As U.S. involvement in Africa increased under the Bush administration, so did the strategic value of a hospitable and relatively stable regime like Djibouti. It is from Djibouti that American forces pursued peacekeeping, counterterrorism, and counterpiracy missions in the Horn of Africa region. The drone involved in the first killing of Al Qaeda militants in Yemen, in 2002, had taken off from Djibouti. While U.S. forces are based in a former camp of the French Foreign Legion, Camp Lemonnier, Djibouti remains host to the largest French contingent in Africa. This strategic rent of military and economic aid paid to the government of Djibouti and the traffic in the seaport help to employ a large number of civil servants and keep the peace between the two majority ethnic groups. The economy has spurred job growth in the service sector: in government, in the foreign bases, and in the seaport.

North of Djibouti, Eritrea licks the wounds of a brutal war of independence under the iron rule of Isaias Afewerki.

In 1951, at the request of the United States, Eritrea and its two seaports—Massawa and Asseb—were gifted by Britain to Ethiopia under a federal arrangement that promised a degree of autonomy to the former Italian colony. But the union rapidly soured, and in 1962 the Ethiopian Negus Haile Selassie imposed direct rule from Addis Ababa just as the Eritrean Liberation Front rose in rebellion. Over the years, the insurgents added the letter P—for People's—to their acronym, after Afewerki, an officer of Christian background, had imposed his Marxist faction over the secessionist movement. The Eritrean People's Liberation Front was armed by Moscow until the reversal of that alliance in 1976, when the Ethiopian *Derg* regime requested support from the Soviet Union.

During the following decade the rebels were on their own. Their ideological colors and reticence toward the West—which in the local political culture had sold them to Ethiopia—prevented an arrangement with the United States, which had briefly considered helping them. The rebels hunkered down. They ran a parastate in the northern mountains and central highlands, burrowed in caves and trenches as any visible movement attracted artillery fire and air raids from Ethiopia's Russian arsenal. Years of drought, the inability to cultivate the land because of land mines, and Ethiopia's obstruction to the delivery of international food aid led to widespread famine in the 1980s. But Eritrea endured, and the rebellion proclaimed independence in 1991 as the regime of Mengistu was overthrown. The United States helped organize a referendum over the issue of partition, and Eritrea's sovereignty was recognized *de jure* in 1993.

At first, the new regime in Addis Ababa cooperated with Eritrea. Meles Zenawi, the new Ethiopian leader, had spent years as a comrade-in-arms to Afewerki, fighting the despotic regime of Mengistu in the Tigray region he hailed from. Both governments tried to work out an arrangement over access to the seaports, but disagreement over the border demarcation ran deep. Full-fledged war resumed in 1998, cutting off Ethiopia from the Eritrean coastline. Borders and reparation issues were referred to the United Nations, but the reconciliation process stalled as Ethiopia rejected the commission's decision. Meanwhile, both countries have used Somalia as a battleground for proxy groups.

Eritrea was born from a long war and after independence remained a country at war. Its history of struggle against Ethiopia in the 1970s and 1980s mirrors that of Somalia. But instead of fragmentation, this is a case where war concentrated power in one institution—the Eritrean People's Liberation Front that won independence and its successor party—and one man—Isaias Afewerki. Afewerki got himself appointed president for life, and his rule since independence has been unequivocally autocratic. There are no alternative political parties, no independent media, no elections, and no civil liberties. Most economic activity is mediated by the state. The devastating war of 1998–2000 tested the resilience of Eritrea, and in a 2001 crackdown Afewerki's close allies were dismissed or arrested for criticizing his bellicose policies and authoritarian attitude. Military camps

enclose prisons, and the prisons of Eritrea are full: diplomatic cables describe cells of 120 square meters—about
1,300 square feet—holding 600 prisoners, including children as young as 8. Their crime often was only to try to
vote with their feet.

Eritrea is a diverse country of 6 million; half of its population is Muslim and the other half Christian. There are two
dominant ethnic Semitic groups and Cushitic minorities.
Afewerki, an elusive man who gives few interviews, has used
this diversity to justify his absolutism, arguing that a closed
political system was necessary to maintain national unity
while the small country was at war against more powerful
enemies.

As expected from a regime with Marxist origins, efforts
have been made to provide basic social services across the
population, in particular with regard to healthcare and education. But the level of investment in human capital and
public infrastructure is inadequate in relation to the growing population, especially since the state is running a deficit
because of high defense expenditures. Agriculture still dom-
inates economic activity, in terms of employment if not of
GDP, which shows the lack of productivity in that sector.
Eritrea survives thanks to the remittances from a large community of refugees. The nature of the regime, its difficult
relationship with Ethiopia, the foreign sanctions imposed
on Eritrea for supporting insurgents are not attractive to
foreign investors.

While the extent of Eritrea's support for Al-Shabab
was debated among diplomats and analysts, Afewerki

vehemently denied any involvement with the Somali jihadists. Whatever the case, the influence of the bankrupt country in regional conflicts should not be exaggerated. But the
violence of those conflicts rests mostly on small arms, and
support does not need to be massive to be consequential.

The contrast in regional aspirations could not be more
striking. While Djibouti is dreaming of becoming a new
Dubai, Somaliland is in search of international recognition,
Somalia is ransacked by violent fundamentalism, Eritrea is
pursuing its rivalry against Ethiopia to the brink of collapse,
and Yemen is teetering on the edge of disaggregation. Militant Islamism has variously affected those Muslim countries, with the cases of Djibouti and Eritrea showing that
strong police states are barren soil in which jihadism cannot grow. Djibouti is remarkable because, although it fits in
the broader regional pattern—ethnic tension, a recent history of civil war, dependency on military aid, a strongman
regime—it also shows that even in that wretched part of the
world, a country can plan a path for development beyond
the exploitation of strategic rent—with the caveat that the
Dubai kind of dream is a flirtation with financial disaster.

For foreign powers, the Horn of Africa is a conundrum.
The geostrategic risk is mitigated by the logistical limitations of the local outfits, their lack of capacity to project
power outside the region. The costs of trying to impose
law and order most certainly outweigh the benefits, at least
in financial terms. As long as local violence does not make
too much of a splash in the global media, foreign governments can look the other way. Even the ransoms paid to

the Somali pirates are not as costly as the upkeep of a large, multinational fleet patrolling a vast swath of the Indian Ocean. The pirates really had to push the envelope in 2008–2009 to provoke a reaction from the international community.

Those whose only vocation has been to push the envelope are the different avatars of Al Qaeda: the original Al Qaeda of the African Embassies and the *USS Cole*, and the new Al Qaeda of the Internet and of the weird stratagems. Those are small clusters of individuals incapable of operating on the scale of an insurgency, but who have a narrow and obsessive focus on throwing down the gauntlet to the United States. The strength of Al Qaeda is not its political claims, its bungled strategic rationale, or its unachievable objectives. Its power rides exclusively on the Al Qaeda brand, forged in the conflagration of 9/11 and universally recognized. Years later, the brand remains a political liability for Western governments. In the world of the twenty-first century, the world of the United Nations, and the world of collective security, mere whiffs of Al Qaeda are a challenge to the fundamental legitimacy of the international state system. It is to keep alive the power of the brand that a handful of jihadists, sheltered in the chaotic region of the Bab el-Mandeb, have remained single-mindedly devoted to killing in the United States and Europe. They are the custodians of the Arabian Sea, the resting place of master global jihadist Osama bin Laden.

There had always been violence in the encounter between Islam and Western powers. Charles Gordon was decapitated at the Battle of Khartoum, and his head presented to his enemy, Mahdi Muhammad Ahmad. Conversely, Gen. Herbert Kitchener, the British victor of the 1898 Battle of Omdurman, which sealed the defeat of the Mahdist state, ordered his men to dispatch wounded Muslim soldiers. Abd al-Kadir, the great hero of the Algerian resistance who was defeated in 1847 and eventually exiled in Damascus, earned international acclaim for protecting Christians in that city during a bout of sectarian violence in 1860. He and his sons walked through the Christian Quarter and invited hundreds to his home, where he promised safety from the mob of Druzes and Kurds. Those were contrasted times when the vicious and the humane, the petty and the magnanimous walked hand in hand.

Zoom forward one century, and the jihad waged by Al Qaeda is grotesquely and irredeemably violent in order to serve a theatrical objective: Al Qaeda has no military power, so it can only strike imaginations. But its gory lethality has had some effect on the ground by redefining the norms of acceptable behavior in the pursuit of political objectives. In the same way that the totalitarianism of the twentieth century legitimized genocidal policies in the pursuit of an ideal society, jihadism has enabled strains of anti-imperialist sentiments in the Muslim world to discard strategic considerations and indulge in gory, apocalyptic carnivals. The trivialization of atrocity has enabled another type of jihadism, one focused internally on the imposition of order through political terror disguised as Islamic tradition and justice. It is the Islam of the veils, the amputations, and the stonings—it is the spirit of the French Revolution under Robespierre, the reign of the guillotine used to force together a society traumatized by revolutions, wars, and deep social change.

Yemen shows symptoms of the first kind of jihadism, Somalia the latter. But as Djibouti and Eritrea show, the main challenge for regional states is not ideology but the economic, environmental, and demographic crises in gestation that could lead to more social dislocation and conflict. In the 1960s and 1970s, current and aspiring regimes across the Bab el-Mandeb flirted with Marxism. But ideological convictions were only skin-deep: Marxism was a tool to handle a society in transition that the rulers did not know how to wield. Human and economic development lagged, and the doctrinal colors eventually dissipated.

From that original failure, things went in different directions. The powers that be retained the autocratic logic of Marxism-Leninism, and they used it to build a rent-based authoritarianism. They used the oil rent when they could, but often had to play a dangerous game exploiting their own potential for disorder in order to extract military and economic aid from foreign powers—the strategic rent on which they have become so dependent. There was a saying about Somalia in the 1990s that there is no business like aid business. The pattern has held.

Meanwhile, the discontents draped the revolutionary logic of Marxism-Leninism in the green of the Islamic tradition and made a bid for political control. Control is a good thing. Law and order are necessary for economic activity, but it depends on what kind of law and what kind of order. Both autocracies and fundamentalism are obsessively political, and they lack the disciplined developmental project that the fragile countries and vulnerable populations of the Arabian Sea need. For Yemen to grow Khat, and for Somalia to specialize in livestock, is an invitation to disaster in the drought-prone region. Herds were wiped out when rain failed in 2011, and people began to starve. The famine would have mostly killed in the Shabab-controlled areas of southern Somalia that aid could not reach. But all the countries of the region were affected by the drought, and their governments exposed for their ineptitude and continued dependence on foreign aid. The *Arabia Felix* of the Romans is no more: in its stead are failed, sad lands from which native populations scramble to emigrate. Djibouti's dreams are pinned on a bridge across the Gates of Tears, but on both shores lie poverty, theft, and violence.

BIBLIOGRAPHY

Sources for Chapter 1: *The Gates of Tears*

Chaudhuri, K.N. *Trade and Civilisation in the Indian Ocean: An Economic History from the Rise of Islam to 1750.* Cambridge: Cambridge University Press, 1985.

Abu-Lughod, Janet L. *Before European Hegemony: The World System A.D. 1250–1350.* Oxford: Oxford University Press, 1991.

Furber, Holden. *Rival Empires of Trade in the Orient, 1600–1800.* Minneapolis: University of Minnesota Press, 1976.

Fradin, Murray S. *Jihad: The Mahdi Rebellion in the Sudan.* Lincoln, NE: Authors Choice Press, 2003.

Green, Dominic. *Three Empires on the Nile: The Victorian Jihad, 1869–1899.* New York, NY: Free Press, 2007.

Kiser, John. *Commander of the Faithful: The Life and Times of Emir Abd el-Kader (1808–1883).* Rhinebeck, NY: Monkfish Book Publishing, 2008.

Haykel, Bernard. *Revival and Reform in Islam: The Legacy of Muhammad al-Shawkani.* Cambridge: Cambridge University Press, 2003.

Algar, Hamid. *Wahhabism: a Critical Essay.* Oneonta, NY: Islamic Publications International, 2002.

Jalal, Ayesha. *Partisans of Allah.* Cambridge: Harvard University Press, 2008.

Sources for Chapter 2: *In the Land of the Mad Mullah: Somalia*

Abdi Elmi, Afyare. *Understanding the Conflagration of Somalia: Identity, Islam and Peacebuilding.* New York, NY: Pluto Press, 2010.

Abdi Elmi, Afyare. "Somali Islamists: A potential ally?" *Al Jazeera online.* January 12, 2010.

Wright, Lawrence. *The Looming Tower: Al-Qaeda and the Road to 9/11.* New York, NY: Knopf, 2006.

U.S. Department of State. "Report of the Accountability Review Boards on the Embassy Bombings in Nairobi and Dar es Salaam on August 7, 1998." January 1999, http://www.state.gov/www/regions/africa/accountability_report.html.

International Crisis Group. "Somalia: Countering Terrorism in a Failed State." Africa Report no. 45. May 23, 2002, http://www.crisisgroup.org/en/regions/africa/horn-of-africa/somalia/045-somalia-countering-terrorism-in-a-failed-state.aspx.

International Crisis Group. "Counter-terrorism in Somalia: Losing hearts and minds?" Africa Report no. 95. July 11, 2005, http://www.crisis group.org/en/regions/africa/horn-of-africa/somalia/095-counter-terrorism-in-somalia-losing-hearts-and-minds.aspx.

International Crisis Group. "Somalia's Islamists." Africa Report no. 100. December 12, 2005, http://www.crisisgroup.org/en/regions/africa/horn-of-africa/somalia/100-somalias-islamists.aspx.

The World Bank. "Conflict in Somalia, Drivers and Dynamics." The World Bank, 2005, http://siteresources.worldbank.org/INTSOMALIA/Resources/conflictinsomalia.pdf.

Menkhaus, Ken. *Somalia: State Collapse and the Threat of Terrorism.* Adelphi paper 364, International Institute for Strategic Studies, 2004, http://www.iiss.org/publications/adelphi-papers/adelphi-papers-archive/ap-364s omalia-state-collapse/.

Choi Ahmed, Christine. "God, Anti-Colonialism and Dance: Sheekh Uways and the Uwaysiyya." In Gregory Maddox, ed., *Conquest and Resistance to Colonialism in Africa.* New York, NY: Garland Publishing, 1993, 145–67.

Samatar, Said S., ed. *In the Shadow of Conquest: Islam in Colonial Northeast Africa.* Trenton, NJ: Red Sea Press, 1992.

Hoehne, Markus Virgil. "Counter-terrorism in Somalia: How external interference helped to produce militant Islamism." Social Science Research Council, 2009, http://webarchive.ssrc.org/Somalia_Hoehne_v10.pdf.

Sii'arag, A. Duale. "The Birth and Rise of Al-Ittihad Al-Islami in the Somali Inhabited Regions in the Horn of Africa." November 13, 2005, http://wardheernews.com/articles/November/13_Alittihad_Sii'arag.ht ml.

Hartley, Aidan. *The Zanzibar Chest*. New York, NY: Atlantic Monthly Press, 2003.

Bowden, Mark. *Black Hawk Down: a Story of Modern War*. New York, NY: Atlantic Monthly Press, 1999.

Bryden, Matt. Update on Situation in Muqdisho, March 29, 1995. University of Pennsylvania—African Studies Center, 1995, http://www.africa.upenn.edu/Hornet/Magdish.html.

Garthoff, Raymond L. *Détente and Confrontation: American-Soviet Relations from Nixon to Reagan*. Washington, DC: Brookings Institution, 1994.

Kapuściński, Ryszard. *The Emperor: Downfall of an Autocrat*. New York, NY: Harcourt Brace Jovanovich, 1978.

Rubin, Barry, ed. *Guide to Islamist Movements*. Armonk, NY: M.E. Sharpe, 2010.

Albin-Lackey, Christopher. "From the Horn of Africa, a Ray of Hope." *The Huffington Post*. July 21, 2010, http://www.huffingtonpost.com/chris-albinlackey/from-the-horn-of-africa-a_b_654514.html.

Eubank, Nicholas. "Taxation, Political Accountability, and Foreign Aid: Lessons from Somaliland." *Journal of Development Studies*, forthcoming. *Social Science Research Network* Web, July 7, 2011, http://ssrn.com/abstract=1621374.

Barnes, Cedric, and Harun Hassan. "The Rise and Fall of Mogadishu's Islamic Courts," Africa Programme Briefing Paper 07/02. London, UK: Chatham House (The Royal Institute for International Affairs), April 2007.

SOURCES FOR CHAPTER 3: *In the Land of the Imam: Yemen*

Mackintosh-Smith, Tim. *Yemen: The Unknown Arabia.* Woodstock, NY: Overlook Press, 2000.

Caton, Steven C. *Yemen Chronicle: an Anthropology of War and Mediation.* New York, NY: Hill & Wang, 2005.

Clark, Victoria. *Yemen: Dancing on the Heads of Snakes.* New Haven, CT: Yale University Press, 2010.

Barendse, R.J. *Arabian Seas 1700–1763: The Western Indian Ocean in the Eighteenth Century.* Leiden, Netherlands: Brill Publishers, 2009.

Um, Nancy. *The Merchant Houses of Mocha: Trade & Architecture in an Indian Ocean Port.* Seattle: University of Washington Press, 2009.

Kerr, Malcom H. *The Arab Cold War: Gamal 'Abd Al-Nasir and His Rivals, 1958–1970.* Oxford University Press, 1971.

Burrowes, Robert D. *The Yemen Arab Republic: The Politics of Development, 1967–1986.* Boulder, CO: Westview Press, 1987.

Dresch, Paul. *A History of Modern Yemen.* New York, NY: Cambridge University Press, 2000.

Brand, Laurie A. *Jordan's Inter-Arab Relations: The Political Economy of Alliance Making.* New York, NY: Columbia University Press, 1995.

Sidahmed, Abdel Salam and Anoushiravan Ehteshami, eds. *Islamic fundamentalism.* Boulder, CO: Westview Press, 1996.

Al-Ghabri, Ismail. "Illiteracy as a major concern to Yemen and the Arab world." *Yemen Times*, January 19, 2009, http://www.yementimes.com/DefaultDET.aspx?i = 1226&p = front&a = 2.

Darem, Faisal. "Yemen Anti-Corruption Commission refers officials to public prosecution." Al-Shorfa.com, December 7, 2010, http://alshorfa.com/cocoon/meii/xhtml/en_GB/features/meii/features/main/2010/12/07/feature-02.

"US Embassy Cables: Saudi Royals Believe Army Rule Better for Pakistan," from the series US Embassy Cables: The Documents. *Guardian*, December 1, 2010, http://www.guardian.co.uk/world/us-embassy-cables-documents/207396.

Burke, Jason. *The True Story of Radical Islam.* London, UK: Penguin, 2004.

Boucek, Christopher and Marina Ottoway, eds. *Yemen on the Brink.* Washington, DC: Carnegie Endowment for International Peace, 2010.

Dresch, Paul. *A History of Modern Yemen.* New York, NY: Cambridge University Press, 2001.

Dresch, Paul. *Tribes, Government, and History in Yemen.* Oxford: Oxford University Press, 1994.

Commins, David. *The Wahhabi Mission and Saudi Arabia.* New York, NY: I.B. Tauris, 2006.

"Building the New (Al-Saleh Republic): Al-Saleh Family Strategies in Ruling the Future Yemen." *Yemen Post.* July 12, 2010, http://yemen post.net/Detail123456789.aspx?ID = 3&SubID = 2399&MainCat = 6.

Schwedler, Jillian. "The Islah Party in Yemen: Political Opportunities and Coalition Building in a Transitional Polity." *Islamic Activism: A Social Movement Theory Approach.* Ed. Quentin Wiktorowicz. Bloomington, Indiana: Indiana University Press, 2004. 205–228.

World Bank. "World Bank's Response to Qat Consumption in Yemen." *Qat Dialogue in Yemen.* Web. July 7, 2011, http://siteresources.world bank.org/INTYEMEN/Resources/YEMEN—WorldBank_Response_ to_QatConsumption.pdf

Ward, Christopher. "Yemen: CDR Building Block Qat." *Comprehensive Development Review,* World Bank, 2000. Web, July 7, 2011, http:// siteresources.worldbank.org/INTYEMEN/Overview/20150264/YE- Qat.pdf.

Sources for Chapter 4: *In the Land of the Mahdi: Sudan*

Evans-Pritchard, Edward E. *The Nuer: A Description of the Modes of Livelihood and Political Institutions of a Nilotic People.* Oxford: Clarendon Press, 1940.

Nkrumah, Gamal. "Sadig Al-Mahdi: The comeback king." *Al-Ahram Weekly Online*, July 15–21, 2004, no. 699, http://weekly.ahram.org .eg/2004/699/profile.htm.

Burr, Milard and Robert O. Collins. *Revolutionary Sudan: Hasan al-Turabi and the Islamist State, 1989–2000.* Leiden, Netherlands: Brill Publishers, 2003.

Gallab, Abdullahi A. *The First Islamist Republic: Development and Disintegration of Islamism in the Sudan.* Hampshire, England: Ashgate, 2008.

Bodansky, Yossef. *Bin Laden: The Man Who Declared War on America.* Roseville, CA: Prima Publishing, 2001.

McCarthy, Andrew C. "Prosecuting the New York Sheikh." *Middle East Quarterly,* March 1997.

Scheuer, Michael. *Through Our Enemies' Eyes: Osama bin Laden, Radical Islam and the Future of America.* Dulles, VA: Potomac Books, 2002.

Gerges, Fawaz A. *The Far Enemy: Why Jihad Went Global.* Cambridge University Press, 2005.

Mayer, Jane. *The Dark Side: The Inside Story of How the War on Terror Turned Into a War on American Ideals.* New York, NY: Anchor Books, 2009.

Mayer, Jane. "Outsourcing Torture: The Secret History of America's 'Extraordinary Rendition' Program." *New Yorker,* February 14, 2005.

"US missed three chances to seize Bin Laden." *The Sunday Times* (U.K.), January 6, 2002, http://www.freerepublic.com/focus/fr/ 602402/posts.

Coll, Steve. *Ghost Wars: The Secret History of the CIA, Afghanistan, and Bin Laden, from the Soviet Invasion to September 10, 2001.* London: Penguin, 2004.

Wright, Lawrence. *The Looming Tower: Al-Qaeda and the Road to 9/11.* New York, NY: Knopf, 2006.

"Bombings connect to mysterious arrests." *Victoria Advocate.* August 13, 1998.

Voll, John O., ed. *Sudan: State and Society in Crisis.* Bloomington, IN: Indiana University Press, 1991.

Miller, Judith. "Faces of fundamentalism: Hassan al-Turabi and Muhammed Fadlallah. " *Foreign Affairs,* November–December 1994.

Viorst, Milton. "Sudan's Islamic Experiment." *Foreign Affairs,* May–June 1995.

Harmony Project. "Cracks in the foundation: Leadership Schisms in al-Qa'ida from 1989–2006." West Point, NY: Combating Terrorism Center at West Point, 2007, http://www.ctc.usma.edu/aq/pdf/Harmony_3_ Schism.pdf.

Burke, Jason. *Al-Qaeda: the true story of radical Islam.* New York, NY: I.B. Tauris, 2004.

Porter, Gareth. "Khobar Towers Investigated: How a Saudi Deception Protected Osama bin Laden." IPS News, June 22–26, 2009, http://www.ipsnews.net/news.asp?idnews = 47376.

National Commission on Terrorist Attacks. *The 9/11 Commission Report: Final Report of the National Commission on Terrorist Attacks Upon the United States.* New York, NY: Norton, 2004, http://www.gpoaccess.gov/911/index.html.

Sageman, Marc. *Understanding Terror Networks.* Philadelphia: University of Pennsylvania Press, 2004.

Sageman, Marc. *Leaderless Jihad: Terror Networks in the Twenty-First Century.* Philadelphia: University of Pennsylvania Press, 2008.

Filiu, Jean-Pierre. "The Brotherhood vs. Al-Qaeda: A Moment Of Truth?" *Current Trends in Islamist Ideology* 9 (November 12), Hudson Institute, 2009, http://www.currenttrends.org/research/detail/the-brotherhood-vs-al-qaeda-a-moment-of-truth.

SOURCES FOR CHAPTER 5: *War at Sea*

"Abu al-Hassan and the Islamic Army of Aden-Abyan." Al-bab.com. January 1999, http://www.al-bab.com/yemen/hamza/hassan.htm.

Eichstaedt, Peter. *Pirate State: Inside Somalia's Terrorism at Sea.* Chicago: Lawrence Hill Books, 2010.

Chalk, Peter. *The Maritime Dimension of International Security: Terrorism, Piracy, and Challenges for the United States.* Santa Monica, CA: RAND Corporation, 2008.

Gettleman, Jeffrey and Michael Gordon. "Pirates' Catch Exposed Route of Arms in Tense Sudan." *New York Times,* December 8, 2010.

Gettleman, Jeffrey. "Money in Piracy Attracts More Somalis." *New York Times,* November 9, 2010, http://www.nytimes.com/2010/11/10/world/africa/10somalia.html?_r = 1&partner = rss&emc = rss.

Lehr, Peter, ed. *Violence at Sea: Piracy in the Age of Global Terrorism.* New York, NY: Routledge, 2006.

Greenberg, M.D., Chalk, P., Willis, H.H., Khilko, I., and Ortiz, D.S. *Maritime terrorism: Risk and liability.* Arlington, VA: RAND Center for Terrorism—Risk Management Policy, 2006.

Middleton, R. *Piracy in Somalia: Threatening global trade, feeding local wars.* Chatham House briefing paper, Africa Programme, October 2008, http://www.icc-ccs.org.

Cawthorne, Nigel. *Pirates of the 21st Century: How Modern-Day Buccaneers are Terrorising the World's Oceans.* London: John Blake, 2009.

International Maritime Bureau. "Piracy and Armed Robbery against Ships, Annual Report 2009." London: International Chamber of Commerce, 2010.

"Plus de quarante migrants se noient au large du Yémen." *Le Monde,* January 3, 2011.

Bowden, Anna. "Oceans Beyond Piracy: The Economic Costs of Maritime Piracy." One Earth Future Foundation Working Paper, 2010, http://oceansbeyondpiracy.org/documents/OBP_Brochure_A4.pdf.

"No stopping them: For all the efforts to combat it, Somali piracy is posing an ever greater threat to the world's shipping." *The Economist,* February 3, 2011.

"At sea: Piracy off the coast of Somalia is getting worse." *The Economist,* February 3, 2011.

SOURCES FOR CHAPTER 6: *The Rise of the Shabab*

"US Embassy Cables: Ethiopian Intelligence Chief Gives Rare Interview," from the series US Embassy Cables: The Documents. *Guardian,* December 8, 2010, http://www.guardian.co.uk/world/us-embassy-cables-documents/210732.

"Islamists half-ready for holy war." *The Economist,* October 12, 2006.

"Hizbullah, Somali Islamists deny UN report alleging cooperation." Beirut, *Daily Star.* November 16, 2006.

Final report of the Monitoring Group on Somalia submitted in accordance with Resolution 1676 (2006), November 22, 2006, S/2006/913, http://www.un.org/sc/committees/751/mongroup.shtml.

Report of the Monitoring Group on Somalia submitted in accordance with Resolution 1853 (2008), March 10, 2010, S/2010/91, http://www.un.org/sc/committees/751/mongroup.shtml.

Report of the Monitoring Group on Somalia submitted in accordance with Resolution 1811 (2008), December 10, 2008, S/2008/769, http://www.un.org/sc/committees/751/mongroup.shtml.

Gettleman, Jeffrey. "In Somali Civil War, Both Sides Embrace Pirates." *New York Times,* September 1, 2010, http://www.nytimes.com/2010/09/02/world/africa/02pirates.html?_r=1.

Amnesty International. "Somalia: Girl stoned was a child of thirteen." Press release, October 31, 2008, http://www.amnestyusa.org/document.php?id=ENGPRE200810317930.

Raghavan, Sudarsan. "In Somalia's War, A New Challenger Is Pushing Back Radical Al-Shabab Militia." *The Washington Post,* May 27, 2010, http://www.washingtonpost.com/wp-dyn/content/article/2010/05/26/AR2010052605279.html.

Shinn, David. "Fighting Terrorism in East Africa and the Horn." *Foreign Service Journal,* September 2004, 36–42.

Menkhaus, Ken. *Somalia: A country in peril, a policy nightmare.* ENOUGH Project strategy paper, September 2008, http://www.enoughproject.org.

Albin-Lackey, Christopher. "So much to fear: war crimes and the devastation of Somalia." New York: Human Rights Watch, December 8, 2008, http://www.hrw.org/en/reports/2008/12/08/so-much-fear-0.

Albin-Lackey, Christopher. "The US Role in Somalia's Calamity." *The Huffington Post*, December 29, 2008, http://www.huffingtonpost.com/chris-albinlackey/the-us-role-in-somalias-c_b_153939.html.

Albin-Lackey, Christopher. "Harsh War, Harsh Peace: Abuses by al-Shabaab, the Transitional Federal Government, and AMISOM in Somalia." New York: Human Rights Watch, April 18, 2010, http://www.hrw.org/en/reports/2010/04/13/harsh-war-harsh-peace.

United States Commission on International Religious Freedom. "The Commission's Watch List: Somalia" annual report, May 1, 2009, http://www.unhcr.org/refworld/publisher,USCIRF,,,4a4f272bc,0.html.

"Two Somali Militant Groups, Once Adversaries, Join Forces and Promise More Attacks." *New York Times*, December 23, 2010, http://www.nytimes.com/2010/12/24/world/africa/24somalia.html? ref=world&pagewanted=print.

Bruton, Bronwyn E. *Somalia: A New Approach*. New York, NY: Council on Foreign Relations Press, 2010.

Menkhaus, Ken. "Violent Islamic Extremism: Al-Shabaab Recruitment in America." United States Senate, hearing before the Committee on Homeland Security and Governmental Affairs, March 11, 2009.

International Crisis Group. "Somalia: To Move Beyond the Failed State." *Africa Report* no. 147, December 23, 2008, http://www.crisisgroup.org/en/regions/africa/horn-of-africa/somalia/147-somalia-to-move-beyond-the-failed-state.aspx.

International Crisis Group. "Somalia's Divided Islamists." *Africa Briefing* no. 74, May 18, 2010, http://www.crisisgroup.org/en/regions/africa/horn-of-africa/somalia/B074-somalias-divided-islamists.aspx.

Le Sage, Andre. "Somalia's Endless Transition: Breaking the Deadlock." *Strategic Forum* no. 257, June 2010, Institute for National Strategic Studies, National Defense University.

Pantucci, Rafaello. "Understanding the al-Shabaab Networks." *Policy Analysis* 49, October 13, 2009, Australian Strategic Policy Institute, http://www.humansecuritygateway.com/documents/ASPI_Somalia_ UnderstandingAlShabaabNetworks.pdf.

Heintz, Vincent G. "Eritrea and Al Shabaab: Realpolitik on the Horn of Africa." *Small Arms Journal*, August 29, 2010.

"Jihad: The End of an Era." *Baobab* blog, *The Economist*, June 14, 2011, http://www.economist.com/blogs/baobab/2011/06/jihad.

SOURCES FOR CHAPTER 7: *Al Qaeda Redux*

Harman, Danna. "Yemen fights own terror war." *The Christian Science Monitor*, February 5, 2002.

Johnson, Gregory. "Yemen's Passive Role in the War on Terrorism." *Terrorism Monitor* 4, 2006, 4–6.

Hegghammer, Thomas. *Jihad in Saudi Arabia: Violence and Pan-Islamism since 1979*. Cambridge University Press, 2010.

Trabelsi, Habib. "Saudi Jihadist accuses Iran of sponsoring Qaeda." Middle East Online. March 30, 2009, http://www.webcitation.org/ query?url = http://www.middle-east-online.com/english/%3Fid%3 D31258&date = 2009-04-11.

Black, Ian. "Yemen terrorism: Soft approach to jihadists starts to backfire as poverty fuels extremism." *The Guardian*, July 30, 2008, http:// www.guardian.co.uk/world/2008/jul/30/yemen.alqaida.

Worth, Robert F. "Is Yemen the Next Afghanistan?" *New York Times*, July 6, 2010.

Amira, Dan. "Pentagon Hosted Future Terrorist Imam for Lunch." *New York* magazine, October 21, 2010, http://nymag.com/daily/intel/ 2010/10/pentagon_hosted_future_terrori.html.

Shane, Scott and Souad Mekhennet. "Imam's Path from Condemning Terror to Preaching Jihad." *New York Times*, May 8, 2010.

Walker, Peter and Johnny McDevitt. "Cargo plane bomb plot tipoff came from ex-Guantánamo Bay detainee." *The Guardian*, November 1, 2010, http://www.guardian.co.uk/world/2010/nov/01/cargo-plane-bomb-plot-tipoff.

"US Embassy Cables: Yemeni President Saleh Rejects US Ground Presence," from the series US Embassy Cables: The Documents. *Guardian*, December 3, 2010, http://www.guardian.co.uk/world/us-embassy-cables-documents/242380.

Sharpe, Tom. "Radical imam traces roots to New Mexico: Militant Islam cleric's father graduated from NMSU." *The New Mexican*, November 14, 2009, http://www.santafenewmexican.com/Local%20News/Radical-imam-traces-roots-to-N-M-.

Knickmeyer, Ellen. "Attack Against U.S. Embassy In Yemen Blamed on Al-Qaeda." *Washington Post*, September 18, 2008.

Schmitt, Eric and Eric Lipton. "Focus on Internet Imams as Al Qaeda Recruiters." *New York Times*, December 31, 2009.

Riedel, Bruce and Bilal Y. Saab. "Al Qaeda's third front: Saudi Arabia." *Washington Quarterly* 31: 2, 2008, 33–46.

Al-Rasheed, Madawi. *Contesting the Saudi State: Islamic Voices From a New Generation*. Cambridge: Cambridge University Press, 2007.

Black, Ian. "Former Guantánamo inmate named as al-Qaida deputy in Yemen." *The Guardian*, January 23, 2009.

Mardini, Ramzy, ed. *The Battle for Yemen: Al-Qaeda and the Struggle for Stability*. Washington, DC: The Jamestown Foundation, 2010.

Trofimov, Yaroslav. *The Siege of Mecca*. New York, NY: Anchor Books, 2008.

Boucek, Christopher. "Saudi Arabia's 'Soft' Counterterrorism Strategy: Prevention, Rehabilitation, and Aftercare." *Carnegie Papers*, Carnegie Endowment for International Peace, 2008, www.carnegieendowment.org/publications/?fa = view&id = 22155.

Lynch, Marc. "Al-Qaeda's Media Strategies." *National Interest*, spring 2006, http://nationalinterest.org/article/al-qaedas-media-strategies-883.

SOURCES FOR CHAPTER 8: *The Sad Lands*

Iyob, Ruth. *The Eritrean Struggle for Independence: Domination, Resistance, Nationalism 1941–1993*. Cambridge: Cambridge University Press, 1995.

International Crisis Group. "Eritrea: The Siege State." *Africa Report* no. 163, September 21, 2010, http://www.crisisgroup.org/en/regions/africa/horn-of-africa/ethiopia-eritrea/163-eritrea-the-siege-state.aspx.

Rémy, Jean-Philippe. "WikiLeaks : la torture et le totalitarisme, quotidien de l'Erythrée, pays à la dérive." *Le Monde*, December 17, 2010.

Sau, Anthony. "Region in Rebellion: Eritrea." *National Geographic*, September 1985, 88.

CAMILLE PECASTAING is a senior associate professor of Middle East studies at the Paul H. Nitze School of Advanced International Studies (SAIS) at Johns Hopkins University. A student of behavioral sciences and historical sociology, his research focuses on the cognitive and emotive foundations of xenophobic political cultures and ethnoreligious violence, using the Muslim world and its European and Asian peripheries as a case study. He has written on political Islam, Islamist terrorism, social change and globalization. He received his PhD in international relations from SAIS.

HERBERT AND JANE DWIGHT
WORKING GROUP ON
ISLAMISM AND THE
INTERNATIONAL ORDER

The Herbert and Jane Dwight Working Group on Islamism and the International Order seeks to engage in the task of reversing Islamic radicalism through reforming and strengthening the legitimate role of the state across the entire Muslim world. Efforts will draw on the intellectual resources of an array of scholars and practitioners from within the United States and abroad, to foster the pursuit of modernity, human flourishing, and the rule of law and reason in Islamic lands—developments that are critical to the very order of the international system.

The Working Group is chaired by Hoover fellows Fouad Ajami and Charles Hill with an active participation of Director John Raisian. Current core membership includes Russell A. Berman, Abbas Milani, and Shelby Steele, with contributions from Zeyno Baran, Reuel Marc Gerecht, Ziad Haider, John Hughes, Nibras Kazimi, Bernard Lewis, Habib Malik, Camille Pecastaing, and Joshua Teitelbaum.

INDEX

Mohamed, Garaad Mohamud, 92
Mohamed, Khalfan Khamis, 79
Mohammed, Fazul Abdullah, 79, 81, 105
Mohammed, Khalid Sheikh, 69, 71–72, 139
  capture of, 84
monotheism, 6
Movement of the Combatant Youth. *See* Harakat al-Shabab Mujahideen
Mubarak, Hosni, 69, 72, 73, 76
Mughal Empire, 4
Mughniyah, Imad, 66
Muhammad, 3
Muhammad, Ali Mahdi, 23, 28
mujahideen, 26, 55, 82, 88
  Arab-Afghan, 66
  Egyptian, 68, 76. *See also* Harakat al-Shabab Mujahideen
mujtahids, 6
Muslim Brotherhood, 14, 33, 48, 64, 67, 74
Mutawakkilite Kingdom, 41, 44

Nabhan, Saleh Ali Saleh, 79, 81, 105
al-Nahdi, Jamal, 70
al-Nashiri, Abd al-Rahim, 86, 87–88, 125
Nasser, Gamal Abdel, 41
Nasserism, 42–43
National Islamic Front, 64, 65
National Liberation Front, 43
National Organization for Defending Rights and Freedom, 56
National Volunteer Coast Guard, 91
nationalism, 7, 12, 15, 26, 148
  of Yemen, 44
NATO, 24, 95
9/11, ix, xi, 86, 136, 139, 155
  hijackers of, 135
nomadic tribalism, 2
al-Numayri, Jafaar, 64

Odeh, Mohammed Saddiq, 79–80
Ogaden, 12, 25
Ogaden War, 17–18
oil, 46, 85
  price of, 83, 88
  Yemen and, 53–54
Operation Atalanta, 95
Operation Desert Fox, 87
Operation Desert Shield, 78
Operation Enduring Freedom, 95
Operation "Ocean Shield," 95

opium, 114
Organization of the Islamic Conference and Islamic League, 65
Oromo Liberation Front, 17
orthopraxy, 115
Ottoman Empire, x, 8, 38
  demise of, 40
Al-Owfi, Mohammed, 128
al-Owhali, Mohamed Rashid, 79

Pakistan, 7
Palestine
  liberation of, 66, 71
  U.S. and, 69
Path of Tradition and Community. *See* Ahlu Sunnah wal-Jama'a
patronage, 45, 54, 130
Pax Britannica, 90
Pax Islamica, 3
Pecastaing, Camille, xiv
Petraeus, David, 140
piracy, 3, 91–92, 94–95, 155
  prosecution of, 97
  publicity of, 93
  Somalia and, 97–98
policy, xiv
politics
  organization of, 15
  of Yemen, 47
Le Ponant, 94
Popular Arab Islamic Conference, 65
population growth, 50
propaganda, 127, 133
proselytism, 8, 29
Protectorate of South Arabia, 43
psychological warfare, 139
Puntland, 21

Qadiriyyah Sufism, 13
Al Qaeda, 53, 69, 80, 82–83, 87–88, 119, 127–29, 132–34, 151, 155–56
  fundamentalism of, 33
  Al-Ittihad al-Islami and, 102
  jihadists of, 55
  Saleh and, 139–41
  al-Shabab and, 114
  shura of, 72
  suicide bombings by, 141
  visibility of, 139
  Yemen and, 123–24
al-Qaradawi, Shaykh Yusuf, 136

Yemen (*continued*)
  modern history of, 41
  Mutawakkilite Kingdom of, 41, 44
  nationalism of, 44
  oil reserves of, 53–54
  politics of, 47
  population growth of, 50
  Al Qaeda and, 123–24
  social situation in, 130
  tribalism of, 40
  water and, 53–54
Yemeni Journalists Syndicates, 57
Yemeni Socialist Party, 43, 46, 48, 49

Young Believers. *See* Al-Shabab al
  Mu'minin
Yousef, Ramzi, 69, 72

Zaidism, 38, 40, 52, 130, 140, 141
al-Zarqawi, Abu Musab, 89, 127
al-Zawahiri, Ayman, 65, 71, 72, 76
Zaydi (Shia), 7
Zazi, Najibullah, 137
Zenawi, Meles, 152
Zheng He, 4
al-Zindani, Shaykh Abdyl Majeed, 48–49,
  138
al-Zumur, Abud, 68